ACHIEVING
GOALS

BEST PRACTICES:
ACHIEVING
GOALS

DEFINE AND SURPASS YOUR
HIGH PERFORMANCE GOALS

KATHLEEN SCHIENLE

4/08

Collins

An Imprint of HarperCollinsPublishers

HarperCollins books may be purchased for educational,
business, or sales promotional use. For information,
please write: Special Markets Department, HarperCollins
Publishers, 10 East 53rd Street, New York, NY 10022.

Produced for HarperCollins by:

HYLAS PUBLISHING
129 MAIN STREET
IRVINGTON, NY 10533
WWW.HYLASPUBLISHING.COM

FIRST EDITION
Library of Congress Cataloguing-in-Publication Data has
been applied for.

ISBN: 978-0-06-114574-2
ISBN-10: 0-06-114574-2

07 08 09 10 11   RRD   10 9 8 7 6 5 4 3 2 1

Kathleen A. Schienle is a writer and principal of Greer Marketing Communications. She has worked for Ernst & Young, Capgemini, System Software Associates, CableData/U.S. Computer Services, and several metro newspapers. She lives in Evanston, Illinois.

Contents

Preface

Why are goals critical to achieving success? What is a smart goal, anyway? How can you set employees up for success by helping them craft the right goals? How does goal-setting make the performance review process less burdensome?

In this book, we distill the wisdom of some of the best minds in the field of performance management to help you achieve more through goal-setting. The language is simple and the design colorful to make the information easy to grasp.

Quizzes help you assess your knowledge of goal-setting and goal management. Case files show how companies have succeeded by setting challenging goals. Sidebars give you a big-picture look at goal-setting and highlight innovative, out-of-the-box solutions worth considering. Quotes from business leaders will motivate you as you face the challenge of setting smart goals for yourself, your employees, and your organization. Finally, in case you want to dig deeper into the topic of performance management and goals, as well as related management issues, we recommend some of the most important business books available. The authors of these books both influence and reflect today's thinking about goal-setting and management issues. Understanding the ideas they cover will inspire you as a manager.

Even if you don't dip into these volumes, the knowledge you gain from studying the pages of this book will equip you to set meaningful and challenging goals and to achieve more—to help you make a difference to your company and in the lives of the people who support you.

THE EDITORS

GOAL-SETTING BASICS

"Goals give you more than a reason to get up in the morning; they are an incentive to keep you going all day."

—Harvey B. Mackay, author of *Swim with the Sharks Without Being Eaten Alive*

S uccessful business people and achievers in all fields use the techniques of goal-setting, a process that helps you decide exactly what you want to accomplish and then helps you systematically chart your course to get there.

Goals provide both long-term vision and short-term motivation. They keep employees focused and make it easier for you and your staff to organize time and resources to take advantage of opportunities. When workers focus and concentrate time, energy, and resources on a single goal, they can achieve amazing things.

THE POWER OF GOALS

Setting goals is a powerful way to boost performance. When you work toward a challenging goal, you feel motivated. Your effort translates into commitment and, ultimately, results. People with clear goals succeed because they know

Behind the Numbers

THE BENEFITS ARE CLEAR

Research on goal-setting in the worlds of athletics and business has shown consistently that it can lead to enhanced performance. One recent analysis of a series of studies showed that goal-setting led to enhanced performance in 78 percent of sport and exercise studies, with moderate to strong effects in all.

SOURCE: *Handbook for Sport Psychology* edited by R. Singer, H. Hausenblas, and C. Janelle (Wiley, 2001). Cited in "Goal Setting" by Lee Crust in *Peak Performance,* www.pponline.co.uk.

where they're going. In fact, organizations with formalized performance management systems have higher profits, better cash flow, stronger employee performance, productivity well above industry averages, less employee turnover, and higher rates of recruiting success.

For Managers

Managing your staff is a continuous cycle of goal-setting, coaching and feedback, evaluation, and reward. When you set goals, decide on a strategy to achieve them, and agree on milestones along the way, you are establishing standards for measuring competency, the development of skills, and other aspects of your workers' on-the-job performance. Through goal-setting, you can involve employees in the organization's strategic direction, motivate them to perform at a higher level, and encourage continuing communication.

Goal-setting and goal management have other benefits. If you and your employees establish and manage goals, then formal performance reviews generally will be better experiences. Having specific and measurable goals eliminates much of the subjectivity from the evaluation process, and with it any sense of unfairness.

Goals become the standards for measuring performance. Then, the formal review—which should no longer have many surprises—is a good opportunity for you and your employees to evaluate their recent work. If employees are achieving their goals, you can reward them. For many employees, the knowledge and growth

Self-Assessment Quiz

YOUR OWN PREPARATION FOR GOAL-SETTING
Read each of the following statements and indicate whether you agree or disagree. Then check your score at the end.

1. I fully believe goal-setting is the basis for success in performance improvement.
   ○ Agree   ○ Disagree

2. I know I can help my team with their goals, but I can't tell them what their goals are.
   ○ Agree   ○ Disagree

3. We can't move forward without having a thorough knowledge of the company's strategy and objectives, even though they are a moving target.
   ○ Agree   ○ Disagree

4. Employees know they can come to me when they feel things are slipping and get real help.
   ○ Agree   ○ Disagree

5. Dreams are part of goal-setting.
   ○ Agree   ○ Disagree

6. My team never worries about surprises at appraisal time.
   ○ Agree   ○ Disagree

7. It's important for me to get—and stay—up to speed on industry trends.
    ○ Agree   ○ Disagree

8. My people don't feel a big need to participate in the office grapevine.
    ○ Agree   ○ Disagree

9. Goal-setting is a negotiation.
    ○ Agree   ○ Disagree

10. My employees are individuals with distinct styles, and I need to approach goal-setting with that in mind.
    ○ Agree   ○ Disagree

Scoring

Give yourself 1 point for every question you answered "Agree."

Analysis

8–10	You have the potential to be highly successful in helping your team set and achieve their goals.
5–7	You could use some work setting goals for you and your team.
0–4	You still have a lot to learn about goal-setting and performance management.

that result from stretching to reach goals are rewarding in themselves.

For Individuals and Teams

When employees are working toward a goal, every day has a mission. Their self-confidence grows as they recognize their ability to take control of their situation—and to reap rewards from their team and their organization for their accomplishments. The satisfaction they derive from this personal growth keeps them energized and motivated, fresh and productive.

• POWER POINTS •

THE POWER OF GOAL-SETTING

Goal-setting is an indispensable tool that gives shape and direction to the work of an individual employee, as well as to a department and organization.

- It allows an organization to track short- and long-term objectives.

- It provides a framework for stating what the individual wants to achieve and what the organization expects from the individual.

- It focuses employees and managers on planning for the future.

- It inspires people to action.

For Organizations

The benefits of setting goals extend not only to individual employees and to you as their manager, but also to your division or organization and its bottom line. This is especially true when individual goals align with organizational goals in response to the realities of the company's industry and marketplace. When everyone in an institution is committed to these larger goals, the results can be powerful, whether the goals involve increased sales and profitability, improved customer service, or the successful integration of two post-merger companies. Strategic planning and the goal-setting that accompanies it can help a mediocre organization become a world-class performer.

Strategic planning is a structured process. Led by enlightened and trained leaders, strategic planning ultimately determines how an organization's resources can organize and direct its progress. The strategic plan guides managers as they set goals for their department and for their individual employees. The better developed the strategic-planning and goal-setting process, the more efficiently the organization will reach its goals.

Why Goals Work

The reasons that goals are effective are persuasive. Goals work in several ways:

By providing a target. One theory of human behavior, developed by Dr. Maxwell Maltz, author of the breakthrough book *Psycho-Cybernetics,* hypothesizes that each individual

CASE *FILE*

GOAL-SETTING AT GE

The story of General Electric under the leadership of CEO Jack Welch is revealing. Early in his tenure, local managers throughout the global company were operating in silos, completely separate from other departments and even from their own teams as they pursued their own agendas without regard for anyone else.

Welch believed that the workplace should be open and collaborative, and that everyone should fully participate, so he led a series of changes—including establishing new goal-setting practices—that transformed the company.

At all levels of the organization, goals were aligned: individual goals supported departmental goals, and the goals for each department supported those of the next corporate level above it. Individual, departmental, and divisional goals all supported goals set at the top, which in turn supported the corporate mission.

SOURCE: *Jack Welch & The G.E. Way* by Robert Slater (McGraw-Hill, 1998).

has a "success mechanism" that is part of the subconscious mind. This success mechanism continually searches for ways to help the individual reach targets and resolve problems. People work and feel better when their success mechanism is fully engaged. All that's needed to activate this mechanism is a target. Without one, the success mechanism lies dormant or—worse—goes after targets that were not chosen consciously. Having goals ensures that your targets represent what is most important to you.

By helping you focus your time and effort. Most people don't have a single focus during their work days or, if they do, it's on whatever happens to have landed on their desk. Goal-setters have learned to put their time, energy, and resources toward a single objective that will help accomplish some larger end. Even if they work toward this goal for a just few hours at a time, they can achieve outstanding results because of the concentration of effort. Goals provide a way to focus and concentrate time and energy on specific and meaningful targets.

By giving you desire, motivation, and persistence. To achieve something worthwhile, you may struggle and fail several times before you reach your target. High achievers pick themselves up after each fall and continue. Why don't they give up? Where do they find the motivation to persist?

Commitment to goals creates a strong sense of purpose, and that's what keeps them going. It has been said that a person with a big enough "why" can handle almost any "what" or "how."

Goals can help you remember your "why" when you are faced with adversity.

By dictating priorities. It's easy to let distractions, trivial tasks, and general busyness fill your work days, or to allow other people's interests to govern your time. Goals—and the missions, visions, and dreams that inspired them—provide a natural framework that clarifies your priorities so that your choices are based on the long-term view of what is most important to you. There are many forks in the road between where you are now and where you want to be, and goals keep you on the right road.

• POWER POINTS •

THE BENEFITS OF GOAL-SETTING

Studies show a tie between goal-setting and superior performance. But how exactly does goal-setting increase performance? It works by:

- Providing a target for your endeavors

- Helping focus your use of time and resources

- Encouraging persistence

- Dictating priorities in your day-to-day activities

- Offering a roadmap for planning your efforts

By giving you a road map. When you are committed to goals, you will use all your resources to accomplish them. For large, seemingly impossible goals, you need to craft a strategy to reach them by establishing milestones, or intermediate goals, that are easier to achieve. Then you can get to work on each piece. Your intermediate goals help you measure your progress and can warn you if you are getting off course. Then you can make adjustments to your plans and overall strategy as you encounter and overcome obstacles and setbacks, and learn from your mistakes.

RESISTANCE TO GOAL-SETTING

A study estimated that only 10 percent of people bother to think about their goals regularly, and that only 1 to 3 percent of people have clear written goals. If goal-setting is such a powerful tool, why don't more people use it? There are many reasons and, as you prepare to set goals with your staff, it's important to understand them. Some people don't have a vision of the future; without that, it's difficult to set goals. Setting goals can help you get what you want, but you have to be clear about what that is before the goal-setting process can work.

What many people don't understand is that goal-setting can improve their relationships with their managers. Employees who already enjoy good communications with their managers think that's enough. They often don't understand that formal, written goals can make a good working relationship even better.

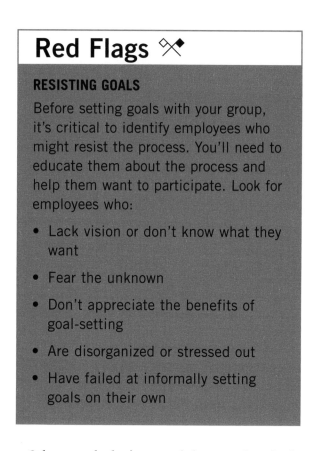

Red Flags

RESISTING GOALS

Before setting goals with your group, it's critical to identify employees who might resist the process. You'll need to educate them about the process and help them want to participate. Look for employees who:

- Lack vision or don't know what they want

- Fear the unknown

- Don't appreciate the benefits of goal-setting

- Are disorganized or stressed out

- Have failed at informally setting goals on their own

Other people don't set goals because they don't comprehend how powerful goals can transform them from good workers to great ones—motivated, successful, and high achieving.

Some workers don't understand the nature of goal-setting. They think they have goals but really just have wishes. Others, who have never used the process properly, simply conclude that goal-setting doesn't work. They don't see goal-setting as a tool that helps them achieve what they want, step by step.

Some people are frightened of goal-setting. The goal-setting process often requires people to overcome their deepest fears—the fear of the unknown and of failure. They are afraid because challenges and risk may take them into unfamiliar, unsafe realms. While adventurous individuals think "nothing ventured, nothing gained," the risk-averse believe "nothing ventured, nothing lost."

> "One of the great discoveries a man makes, one of his great surprises, is to find he can do what he was afraid he couldn't do"
>
> —Henry Ford
> founder of the Ford Motor Company
> (1864–1947)

Some people are too busy and disorganized to spend the time to set goals. They reject the prospect at a subconscious level and come up with excuse after excuse for not setting goals. Already stressed and overwhelmed by the current demands on their time and energy, they are not ready to take on new challenges. They don't understand that having goals will make their lives easier, not more difficult, and will save them time in the long run.

Still other people, feeling inspired, grab a piece of paper, start to list a few goals, then can't decide what to include. They may try to juggle everything they want in all the different areas of their life before committing to any one thing, or they may come up with too many goals and quickly realize they can't handle them all. Feeling frustrated and overwhelmed, they abandon their goals before they even get started—and blame the whole process as defective rather than their approach to it.

MANAGER AS COACH

Not so long ago all managers operated on the command-and-control model, where the boss called the shots, not just for the business but also for individual employees. Today, though many managers still find it difficult to shed the vestiges of this old-school behavior, the coaching method of management is increasingly popular.

The coaching model is grounded in a belief in the innate abilities of people and in the value of their ideas. The focus is on developing skills within the group in order to move the company toward its immediate objectives and long-term goals. Managers who operate like coaches are open and approachable. They involve everyone in setting the goals and objectives for the team and invest time and effort in building relationships with their team members. They are empathetic about setbacks and help remove obstacles to achieving goals. They view their own role as serving the people they work with.

> "Man is a goal-seeking animal. His life has meaning only if he is reaching out and striving for his goals."
>
> —Aristotle,
> Greek philosopher
> (384–322 BCE)

When you make yourself your employees' coach and invest your time in their well being, you counter their resistance to goal-setting more easily. To make goal-setting take hold and become a part of the fabric of your work environment, you have to make it your priority. You also need to communicate and demonstrate the benefits of goal-setting to each individual and to the group as a whole. Ultimately, their success reaching goals will encourage your staff to make goal-setting a part of their lives.

DEVELOPING GOALS THAT WORK

"We overestimate what
we can accomplish
in one year, but we
underestimate what we
can accomplish in five."

—Peter Drucker,
management guru and author
(1909–2005)

As a manager, you will develop goals for your employees, team, department, division, and company. But you should also set goals for yourself. Creating goals that improve performance takes more planning and thought than most people realize.

Although the concept of setting goals may be easy to grasp, many managers don't know

DEFINING THE TERMS

To understand why goal-setting matters to an organization, it's important to distinguish the differences among mission, goal, objective, and task.

Mission – A concise statement that expresses why an organization exists and why it matters, what work it does, for whom and how, and where it's going. Many corporate mission statements also encompass the company's relationship with its employees—how they relate to each other and to their work and sometimes even how they are coached, trained, and rewarded.

Goal – A specific, measurable achievement that helps a company fulfill its mission.

Objective – An action or activity that helps achieve long-range goals.

Task – An "action item" essential to accomplishing an objective and reaching a goal.

THE BOTTOM LINE

how to do it. Personal development coach Gene Donohue, founder of the online motivational site Top Achievement, believes that "the difference between a goal and a dream is the written word." Real goal-setting goes beyond simply drawing up a list of wishes such as the New Year's resolutions that many people—however well intentioned—give up on before the end of January. If you focus only on these wishes or dreams, you can become overwhelmed or discouraged when you think about what it will take to achieve them, and then you might give up on them prematurely.

Although dreams are powerful motivators, goals must be specific, realistic, and achievable. Also, to be effective, they need to be broad and exciting. When you focus on a goal, you should feel motivated, energized, and ready to spring into action. At the same time, the goal must be modest enough to be within your reach. Finally, the problem is often not the goal you set for yourself, but how you follow-up on it. Breaking down challenging goals into smaller goals and tackling them one at a time makes even large goals attainable.

WHAT MAKES GOALS SMART?

Many guidelines for developing powerful goals have been created since the 1950s, when the late Peter Drucker, known as "the father of modern management," first began writing about the philosophy of "management by objectives" (MBO). Many workers and their managers use this method to plan their work for the year in alignment with company goals. By setting objectives with a manager, employees know what's expected and how to get there. When a manager talks about goals with employees, the door is opened to discussions about how these workers are contributing to the company and developing as staff members.

The most widely accepted rule for effective goal-setting is committing the goals to paper in a way that is clear, straightforward, and understandable, and that highlights the actions

The **BIG** Picture

MANAGEMENT BY OBJECTIVES

Management guru Peter Drucker coined the term "management by objectives," or MOB, in his 1954 classic book *The Practice of Management.* He proposed that a company could achieve its best results by articulating specific objectives and a timeline for achieving them—and by writing them down. Drucker also introduced the SMART criteria, which advised that objectives should be Specific, Measurable, Achievable, Realistic, and Time-bound.

Source: *The Practice of Management* (Reissue Edition) by Peter Drucker (Collins, 2006).

required to achieve them. Drucker's formula asserts that goals should be SMART—Specific, Measurable, Achievable, Realistic, and Time-bound—and legions of business leaders since then have agreed.

Taking ownership of ambitious goals helps employees see themselves as worthy of achieving those goals. By stretching to succeed, they develop new skills and confidence. Goals that meet the SMART criteria stand a good chance of being achieved.

Effective Goals Are Specific

When setting goals for yourself or your staff, strive for more, rather than less, detail. Be specific about what steps need to be taken to achieve them. For every goal, answer these questions: Who will be involved in achieving the goal? Where and how will the goal be tackled? What resources—time, money, logistical support, or additional training—will be required? What tasks need to be done to get there? What are the benefits of accomplishing the goals? By when should the goal be met?

Based on the answers to these questions, craft a goal statement in clear, simple language. In the future, if you or your employees seem to have lost the way in pursuit of the goal, you can revisit the goal statement to get back on track.

Effective Goals Are Measurable

To be effective, a goal needs to state what you want to accomplish in a way that can be measured. Otherwise, how will you know when the goal is reached? As you develop goals, consider all tangible evidence of a goal's completion. If quality is a factor, for example, note the standards for measuring it. That way, when your long-range goal is to increase productivity, you can prevent any slide in quality, since the goal statement includes that as a measurement.

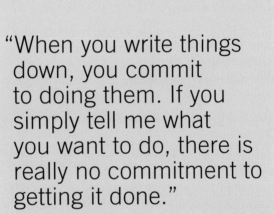

"When you write things down, you commit to doing them. If you simply tell me what you want to do, there is really no commitment to getting it done."

—David Cottrell,
author of *Monday Morning Mentoring*

In the goal statement, also incorporate or suggest benchmarks—medium-range objectives that will indicate progress toward the goal. These concrete indicators make it easier to stay on track and to see forward movement, which can motivate workers to persist when they face difficulties and setbacks.

Can you see or count the results you're aiming for, and compare them to earlier outcomes? Can dreams and expectations be translated into tangible sales or production numbers or process improvements? In this way you can demonstrate real progress or professional development.

Make sure the measurements in your goal-setting statement are clearly defined. "Meet deadlines" is vague, with no specifics or direction, but "Meet nine production deadlines out of the ten scheduled during the next six months, including all specified deliverables" has a time frame and is measurable. "Learn Power-Point fundamentals and be able to produce ten formatted slides an hour by May 1" is also specific and measurable, either as a benchmark on the way to the final goal or as a goal in its own right.

Finally, make sure that your employees understand how their progress toward their goals will be measured during their performance reviews.

Effective Goals Are Action-Oriented and Agreed-Upon

An effective goal inspires action. The goal statement not only communicates the purpose of the goal but also urges the employee along the road to achievement. Consider each goal statement carefully to make sure it is a call to action.

Does the goal statement explain what needs to be done and why? Does it outline concrete steps to take? Will the goal statement motivate others to work toward the same goal? Well-crafted goal statements foster a sense of community and collaborative effort.

To set effective goals, both you and your employee must agree on them. Sticking with a goal's challenge over the long haul takes a deep commitment. Goals mandated by the boss rather than created collaboratively with employees—taking into account their hopes and plans—may not inspire the necessary dedication.

Effective Goals Are Realistic

Realistic goals take into account the availability of resources and the likelihood of roadblocks, distractions, conflicts, and other demands on employees' time. Realistic goals also make the best use of an employee's ambitions and skills for the organization's overall goals and strategy. Even then, the goals should not necessarily be easy to achieve. The best goals are slightly out of reach and require a stretch; your employee may even feel a bit intimidated by them.

Paradoxically, a higher goal, and one of significance to you and your employee, can be more realistic than a lesser goal, because it can inspire greater effort. On the other hand, a goal that's too far out of reach may defeat employees rather than motivate them. Set goals that are ambitious—but not so ambitious that there is little hope of achieving them.

To determine how realistic a goal is, consider several factors. Is the goal challenging enough?

• POWER POINTS •

THE MOST EFFECTIVE GOALS
Some goals stall at the gate, while others take off for success. The most effective goals:

- Are written down
- Specify what steps need to be taken
- Inspire action
- Have a measurable outcome
- Are agreed upon by employees and their managers
- Are ambitious but realistic
- Include a deadline

Even better, is it inspiring—will your employee want to work toward it, even to make sacrifices for it? Given the available time and resources, is the goal likely to be reached? What conditions are necessary to achieve it? Has the employee achieved a similar goal before?

Another important consideration is the employee's control over the situation. If a goal depends on a motivated individual's personal performance, success is likely. But if achieving the goal depends on circumstances outside the worker's control, you may not be able to predict the outcome reliably. Does the goal statement account for unexpected events? Do you have a fallback plan?

Effective Goals Are Time-Bound

Even without a deadline, a goal might be accomplished eventually. But if you don't set a specific date for reaching the goal, your employees may feel little impetus to move ahead and might postpone their work toward that goal. Goal-setting is not static: a manager should always be setting goals, watching employees achieve them, and moving on to new ones. The result is forward movement—whether new achievements or the mastery of new skills.

Set deadlines according to the sequence of events required to complete the goal. To gauge your progress, establish interim deadlines for key accomplishments along the way to the main goal. Similarly, it is also important to set cost and resource parameters so that you keep your planning concrete and realistic.

MANY TYPES OF GOALS

So far, this chapter has discussed the general qualities of effective goals. Next, where can you get ideas for specific goals for individual employees? Your workers may have their own goals, reflecting their life and career ambitions. However, you should consider what you need to target as well. Sometimes, because of a corporate mandate or because of an individual's deficiencies, the goals you need to set are obvious. Otherwise you should look for potential

CASE *FILE*

WORKERS MAKE THEIR OWN CHANGES

After a new "lean" was put into place at Flexible Steel Lacing Co., a Chicago-area manufacturer of conveyor belt fastening systems, its 240 employees were assigned the goal of initiating four improvements each year. Employees who achieved this goal would be able to earn a year-end bonus. This approach to the workplace, with employees in charge of improving processes and encouraged to make decisions on the spot, constituted a huge shift from an earlier culture of managerial entitlement. But the results were striking. In 2006, when workers were coached to think for themselves and not wait for directions, customer delivery times were 36 percent faster than in 2002. When this new efficiency eliminated jobs, workers were retrained and moved into other positions.

SOURCE: "Workers Contribute to Bottom Line" by Ann Meyer, *Chicago Tribune* (August 14, 2006).

improvements in four main areas: performance, individual competency, core competency, and personal development.

Performance Goals

Performance goals are the most obvious to define. They describe the work the employee is expected to turn in, produce, or deliver, as well as specific contributions to the company's business objectives. If a large grocery chain aims to improve its service and ease-of-use, for example, then the goal of a stock person in the produce department might be to create more readable signage, which would be measurable by increased produce sales and fewer questions and complaints from customers.

Performance goals can also encourage people to stretch in their work, to exceed the expectations outlined in their original job descriptions. Note that, if the overall business cycle changes, or an employee is given a new work assignment, performance goals must be adjusted accordingly.

Individual Competency Goals

An employee's "individual competencies" are the knowledge and skills needed to do the work laid out in the job description. During the goal-setting process, consider how the individual employee measures up in key areas: What competencies is the employee lacking? Performance skills or people skills, for instance? Specific knowledge? On the other hand, are there particular strengths that can counter the employee's weaknesses? Competency goals allow employees to focus on their technical skills but provide a unique opportunity to also improve soft skills—personal skills and attitudes, effective communication, ability to think outside the box, flexibility, change-readiness, problem solving, team building, and social dexterity—which are often just as important for success.

Core Competency Goals

Some firms aim to develop their "core competencies"—that is, the unique mix of skills that provides distinct benefits to the company's customers and distinguishes the company in

---

Dos & Don'ts ☑

SET GOALS EFFECTIVELY

These broad guidelines will help you and your employees set effective goals together.

- ☐ Do create today's goals with a larger vision in mind.

- ☐ Do focus on performance goals.

- ☐ Do keep goals concrete, rather than abstract.

- ☐ Don't let fear of failure keep your goals too small.

- ☐ Do remind employees that a belief that a goal is unrealistic may be mistaken.

- ☐ Don't set goals for situations your workers can't control.

The BIG Picture

IMPROVING SOFT SKILLS THROUGH COMPETENCY GOALS

Because soft skills—competencies in the areas of personal attitudes, communication, and social dexterity—are often seen as less important than the technical skills required to succeed at a job, many managers fail to develop them in their employees. But soft skills are the secret ingredient of high-performers: people with strong soft skills work better with others, navigate office politics more diplomatically, and manage their time and resources more effectively. Setting competency goals that allow employees to improve their soft skills can have a positive, long-term effect on your team's overall performance.

Here are some soft skills to consider when setting competency goals:

Initiative and creativity – How much supervision does the worker require? Is this employee highly motivated, eager to tackle new projects, creative about devising new solutions to the same old problems, and conscientious about dealing with issues before they turn into problems?

Leadership and independence – Does this person have a positive influence on others, make sound decisions, and handle snafus independently, or always look for help to get bailed out?

People skills – Is the employee a fair and honest team player, communicating well with peers, subordinates, and managers, and working well with people outside your department and the company?

Productivity – Is this worker a good manager of time and work, able to set priorities, to create tasks and to-do lists, and to execute them? How does his or her productivity compare to that of other workers?

Quality – Is the employee's work complete, accurate, executed at a proper level of detail, and carefully planned and organized? Do you see both consistency and excellence in the employee's work?

Responsibility – Is the employee punctual, reliable, and dependable in following through and meeting deadlines? Is attendance an issue?

the marketplace. Black & Decker's core competency is producing a certain type of motor, for example. A company's core competencies usually reflect the organization's culture and values.

The goal-setting process is an opportunity to discuss your company's core competencies with your employees and in that way to reinforce the corporate culture and values. You should consider how their skills contribute to the firm's core competencies and, if necessary, set higher goals for their performance in those areas.

• POWER POINTS •

THE FOUR TYPES OF GOALS

There are many types of goals. Some goals target specific improvements in performance; some are more general career or organizational goals. Goals that further the success of the company and goals that focus on personal development often can overlap. Most goals fall into the following general categories:

- **Performance Goals** – Goals that define what an employee is expected to produce on the job. They can inspire employees to exceed management's expectations and to improve their overall performance.

Goals Relating to Personal Development

Many goals identify areas for additional personal growth and improvement. These goals include short-term targets, as well as strengthening skills and abilities needed for the next career step.

When setting long-term goals, make sure to include one extremely ambitious goal. Many business leaders have nicknamed these BHAGs—"big, hairy, audacious goals." To help accomplish BHAGs, you might set as smaller

- **Individual Competency Goals** – Goals that help employees develop or improve the skills necessary to do their jobs, as well as to succeed both personally and professionally.

- **Core Competency Goals** – Goals that focus on developing a company's distinctive products, or strengths, by setting the bar high for employees' performance in particular areas.

- **Personal Development Goals** – Goals, both short- and long-term, that target areas for growth and improvement, such as acquiring new skills or eradicating unproductive behaviors.

goals for your employees a specific accomplishment or the acquisition of a new skill. You might focus on improving how an employee performs a routine task, such as preparing a monthly report. Other goals could encourage innovative solutions to problems, such as new ways to make visitors to the company feel

> "You can't get to the top of Everest by jumping up the mountain. You get to the mountaintop by making incremental steps. Step by step you get to the goal."
>
> —Robin Sharma, author of *The Greatness Guide*

more welcome and better-informed. Workers should try to set goals according to their level of motivation, since motivation drives action, and action is the path to achieving goals.

You also can develop goals that help employees manage their work life—for example, restrict the time spent answering e-mail to an hour every day, or complete expense reports each week. Personal development goals can also target bad habits—your staffer might resolve not to miss a deadline, answer the cell phone during staff meetings, or call in sick after a late night.

Some people find it helpful to set one goal with different priorities for different levels of achievement. For instance, assign top priority to meeting one new development prospect every day, medium priority to meeting three a week, and low priority to meeting a minimum of one new person every week. However it's structured, the importance of any goal is that in energizing your employee it helps you both get where you want to go.

THE MANAGER'S ROLE IN SETTING GOALS

"Employees get fired up about their goals if they have a hand in shaping them."

—Tom Gegax,
author of *The Big Book of Small Business*

Not that many years ago, individual goal-setting in the workplace went like this: the CEO called a meeting of the senior leadership team the day after the quarterly vision-mission retreat with top corporate management.

At the meeting, the CEO outlined the corporate goals and objectives for the next fiscal year, then instructed the senior staff to meet with their teams to disseminate the goals and "get all your people onboard!"

Implicit in this command, as senior staff knew from experience, was the need to increase company earnings and get the stock price up. The following day, managers met with their teams, passed out copies of the corporate goals, and warned that performance reviews would be based on how well employees' work supported these goals. Pay increases and promotions would be hanging in the balance.

This top-down method of setting goals sprang from top managers' vision, their need for control, and their sense of obligation to the board or stockholders. The results were often lackluster. To achieve business goals requires the efforts of all employees, and their commitment is indispensable. They are the ones who envision the products, develop the models, build the items, staff the call center, and develop the marketing campaigns. Without their motivation and dedication to accomplishing designated business goals, those goals are unattainable.

Today, managers know that goal-setting from the top down results in lukewarm commitment and weak participation in corporate goals, initiatives, and decisions.

Employees now have a greater sense of their own value and know they have more control over their careers. Just as they no longer expect to spend their lives at one company, they no longer accept paternalistic approaches to management. A purely top-down approach can cause problems with employees, such as poor

THE MANAGER'S ROLE IN GOAL-SETTING

As a manager, one of your most important responsibilities is making sure that goals are met successfully. Achieving business goals requires everyone's effort and commitment. Taking an active role in goal-setting—being clear about the company's mission and helping your employees create their goals—will bring you closer to meeting them. The manager's participation in setting goals should include:

- Ensuring that employees' goals align with corporate goals

- Steering employees toward high but achievable goals

- Identifying and resolving any potential conflict with the goals of employees in other divisions

- Determining how performance will be evaluated and goal achievement measured

- Being an advocate for employees throughout the process

THE BOTTOM LINE

morale, communication, and performance; high turnover; mere lip-service being paid to objectives; and high stress.

So while devising goals for your individual employees and team may take less time, you lose the power of the strong commitment from your workforce you get when each worker is involved. Helping to create the goals gives each employee a personal stake in the outcome. Moreover, when you set goals for the group alone in your office, you forego the insight and experience gained from group synergy, creativity, and diverse perspectives.

On the other hand, when goals are established bottom-up—that is, independently of the rest of the organization by employees at lower levels—there is no guarantee they will meet the needs of senior management and the organization as a whole. Bottom-up processes in general are challenging and time-consuming. Some employees have never been involved in such decisions and don't even know what a goal looks like. Others have been exposed to the approach but without success; they may hold back for fear that it's a trick or trap of some sort. On the other end are those eager for a chance to be heard in the workplace and who are likely, at first, to be all over the map with their suggestions and pronouncements.

The only way to ensure that the expectations of leadership, boards, and stockholders are met, and that employees take ownership of them, is participation throughout the company in setting and meeting goals. When all levels of employees—from the CEO's office to the mail-room—are involved then everyone is aiming for mutual success.

Thus, one of your main responsibilities as a manager is to be clear about the goals of the company and how they might affect individuals and work groups under your supervision. Managers should take an active role in goal-setting from beginning to end, ensuring first that the agreed-upon goal aligns with the corporate, division, or team mission; and second, that everyone involved agrees on the desired outcome.

RESOLVING CONFLICTS IN GOAL-SETTING

What if your company leadership remains unenlightened and sticks to the top-down approach to setting goals? Are you and your team doomed to drudgery? Have you been set up for failure? Even if you didn't have a role in developing a goal, it is still yours to execute if your manager says it is. How, then, do you get motivated to tackle it, and in turn motivate your staff to help?

First, encourage employees to accept the goal as their own and focus on what they can accomplish at their level of responsibility. Urge them to give the goal all the energy, enthusiasm, time, and commitment they would give a goal that was set with their participation. Then, have them adapt the goal by pinpointing key aspects they can achieve. For example, if you've been assigned to bolster your sector's sales quota, ask each employee to set a goal focused on achieving their part of the sales quota and to keep in mind the bonus you will all reap when the overall projections are attained.

Even when your company's top managers embrace a collaborative approach to goal-setting, encouraging you and your employees to participate in setting goals that support the company's strategies, goals might not be synchronized from one department or division to another. Unsynchronized goals can create major conflicts for individual employees or departments caught in the crossfire.

For example, the marketing group's decision to reduce costs by cutting out trade shows undermines the goals of the training team, which had decided to channel all learning for the year through trade show opportunities. What can you do? After setting goals with individual employees, present their goals to your boss, who in turn can compare them with goals in other groups to make sure there are no surprises.

As much as possible, make sure that your own employees' goals support your managerial goals, which in turn must support those of the manager above you. All goals must align with each other and with the corporate strategy, yet be specific to each individual or team as well.

THE GOAL-SETTING PROCESS

Effective goal-setting is a negotiation, with three phases to the process:
(1) the discussion, or detailed presentation of the desired goal and the expected outcome;

WORK **FLOW** TOOLS

COMPANY-WIDE
GOAL PLANNING PROCESS

TOP MANAGERS DEVELOP
A STRATEGY

STRATEGY IS ANNOUNCED
TO TEAMS

MANAGERS AND EMPLOYEES
COLLABORATE ON SETTING GOALS

MANAGERS AND EMPLOYEES
REFINE GOALS

EMPLOYEES CREATE GOAL
STATEMENTS

MANAGERS CONFIRM AGENDA

Outside the Box

THE GROUND RULES

The manager should create an environment conducive to communication in the goal-setting process. Your insistence on the following ground rules is key. Everyone involved must:

- Participate in all group discussions
- Communicate openly and honestly
- Challenge each other's ideas
- Respect each other's expressed views
- Provide constructive feedback
- Give the discussion their undivided attention (cell phones off, no interruptions, etc.)

(2) the compromise, or give-and-take among participants about all aspects of the goal; and (3) the agreement, when everyone commits to the goals to be achieved.

First, hold one-on-one meetings with each of your employees to communicate corporate goals and their component parts. During this discussion, steer employees to set goals in areas where their individual accomplishments will make the greatest contribution to the overall plan. Discuss how each employee's performance contributes to the results you want to achieve. Talk about goals that might be difficult—though still possible—to accomplish and set three or four of them together. Setting high but achievable goals results in higher levels of performance than if you set vague goals or do not set any at all.

Second, define and negotiate tasks to be accomplished that will produce these results. Settle on a time frame for achieving these results. Then, prioritize these goals. Ranking goals helps employees keep each goal's relative importance in mind as they make daily choices and decisions. Wrap up the conversation by discussing how performance will be assessed based on progress toward the goals. If some goals require a group effort, show each team member how individual achievements will contribute to the group's work and how these contributions will be measured. If success achieving a goal will be evaluated by multiple criteria—such as client satisfaction, quality, value added, cost, and quantity, for example—define that clearly.

Third, get your employees to commit to the agreed-upon goals. Without this commitment, setting a goal is pointless.

Once you've completed the three-part process, let your employees know that you will track and update goals along the way. Follow up by monitoring progress and communicating your appreciation or encouragement throughout the year. Be your employee's advocate from beginning to end during the goal-setting and performance evaluation cycle.

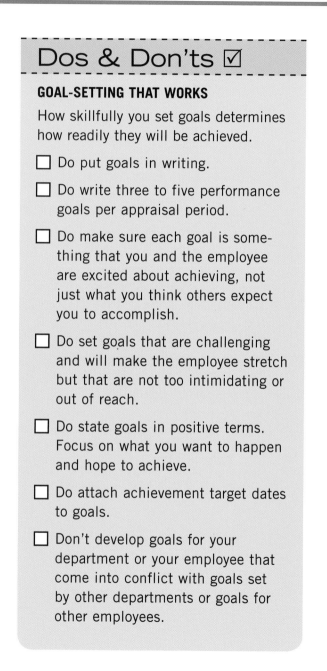

Dos & Don'ts ☑

GOAL-SETTING THAT WORKS

How skillfully you set goals determines how readily they will be achieved.

☐ Do put goals in writing.

☐ Do write three to five performance goals per appraisal period.

☐ Do make sure each goal is something that you and the employee are excited about achieving, not just what you think others expect you to accomplish.

☐ Do set goals that are challenging and will make the employee stretch but that are not too intimidating or out of reach.

☐ Do state goals in positive terms. Focus on what you want to happen and hope to achieve.

☐ Do attach achievement target dates to goals.

☐ Don't develop goals for your department or your employee that come into conflict with goals set by other departments or goals for other employees.

Make an effort to maintain support from upper management in the process, to clarify corporate goals as they evolve, to free up resources for your team, and to help them overcome any barriers to their success.

In addition, plan to celebrate employees' achievements. It's a mistake to involve your people in setting goals and then fail to acknowledge reaching them. If possible, tie at least some part of your workers' salaries, bonuses, or perks (such as training) to their successful achievement of goals you have set together. When employees who meet their goals are treated the same as employees who don't, workers become disgruntled and demoralized, and employee turnover can result.

• POWER POINTS •

THREE PHASES OF GOAL-SETTING

Goal-setting is a vital part of the cycle of managing your employees. The cycle has three phases:

Discussion – A detailed presentation of the desired goal and expected outcome to all participants

Compromise – All participants negotiate all aspects of the goal

Agreement – A commitment to achieve the goals within certain parameters (deadlines, resources, etc.)

Individualizing Goals

One of the serious defects of most top-down goal-setting processes is that they don't consider—and therefore can't maximize—the potential of the person assigned the goal. Unless employees have the right skills, aptitude, and knowledge to accomplish the goals assigned to them, they will not be able to accomplish them.

Research shows that many workers who enjoy what they do actually work for companies that capitalize on employees' strengths. When companies and employees focus on strengths, productivity, employee loyalty, and low turnover follow. But when they focus on weaknesses (which can become a self-fulfilling prophecy), negative attitudes and poor performance follow. The best companies, thus, prevent failures by improving weaknesses, and produce success by developing strengths.

A discipline called SWOT analysis can be helpful in assessing the strengths and weakness of employees and in creating goals that are specifically suited to them. SWOT is an acronym that recommends that you build on your Strengths and resolve your Weaknesses, exploit your Opportunities, and avoid Threats in pursuit of your goals:

Strengths and weaknesses. Start by looking at strengths and weaknesses—your employees', your organization's, and your own. Think about your employees' innate skills and resources. Consider what areas of work are involving and absorbing—where are challenges met with instinctive understanding and an innate grasp? What parts of the job are easy? Which are done with difficulty and inadequately? How does the employee (or the team) fit into the larger organization? What are your employees specifically good at? For example, people handle details differently: Are your employees strong planners or detail-oriented? Are they better at planning or better at executing?

> "To understand the heart and mind of a person, look not at what he has already achieved, but at what he aspires to."
>
> —Kahlil Gibran,
> author of *The Prophet*
> (1883–1931)

Consider strengths realistically, from an internal perspective and from the point of view of your customers and experts in your field. Also, compare your employees' strengths to those of others. What does each of your employees do better than anyone else? What advantages does

Outside the Box

EMOTIONAL INTELLIGENCE AND GOAL-SETTING

To perfom efficiently as a team, coworkers need to interact well with each other. In fact, many employees who are successful at developing strong working relationships and at earning respect and success do so because of their abilities to empathize, motivate themselves, persevere, control impulses, communicate clearly, make thoughtful decisions, solve problems, take criticism and improve, and support their colleagues' efforts in pursuit of their goals.

What underlies these abilities is emotional intelligence—the capacity to perceive, assess, and manage one's own emotions as well as those of others and of groups. Emotional intelligence (also known as EI) was originally named by psychologist Wayne Payne in the mid-1980s and popularized in 1995 by best-selling writer and psychologist Daniel Goleman, who argues that emotions play a crucial role in everyday life and at work and that people can enhance their emotional competency.

Optimism is one aspect of emotional intelligence that leads to increased productivity. New salesmen at Metropolitan Life Insurance who scored high on a test of "learned optimism" sold 37 percent more life insurance in their first two years than did pessimists.

People in your group who have high emotional intelligence are more likely to embrace goal-setting. Before you help team members develop goals, assess their emotional competence. If they are lacking EI, the goal-setting process may be more difficult. If you feel that expanding their EI would improve their performance, advocate for EI training when you are establishing goals. Your human resources department may already have EI training available or could bring in an expert for a staff development day or recommend online coursework.

SOURCE: "The Business Case for Emotional Intelligence" by Cary Cherniss, Consortium for Research on Emotional Intelligence in Organizations, Rutgers University, 2004.

• POWER POINTS •

SWOT ANALYSIS

An acronym for Strengths, Weaknesses, Opportunities, and Threats, SWOT analysis is an approach to goal-setting and decision-making that capitalizes on an organization's strengths. Goals are individualized to take advantage of each employee's potential and are based on a realistic assessment of opportunities and threats.

- Make a comparative analysis of the strengths and weaknesses of your employees.

- Examine the performance of your employees as a team and your own performance as manager.

- Consider the difficulties and chal- lenges of the job and tailor goals accordingly.

- Focus on opportunities in develop- ing performance targets.

- Analyze weaknesses and threats as realistically as possible. It is best to face them upfront when setting goals.

your team have? Are there any unique or low-cost resources you can access?

Also examine your weaknesses both from the inside and from an external viewpoint: Do other people perceive weaknesses in your employees that you don't see? Are other teams doing better than you are? It's best to be realistic now—and to face unpleasant truths when you can do something about them.

Opportunities. Helping employees develop performance targets is all about finding and focusing on the opportunities that are likely to excite them. Opportunities emerge from the specific strengths of your employees and their role in the organization.

Externally, opportunities often arise from change: in technology, markets, government policy, and cultural and lifestyle trends. What are the opportunities facing your employees? What interesting trends do you recognize that you, your employee, or your company could take advantage of? Also, analyze the weaknesses you've identified in your employees and yourself and consider whether eliminating them would unlock any opportunities.

Threats. An analysis of possible threats can be particularly illuminating, not only because it shows what needs to be done, but also for the perspective it offers on your problems. For example, is evolving technology changing the requirements of your employees' jobs—and the goals you should be setting for them? Could any of your employee's weaknesses seriously threaten their—and your ability—to meet the goals you've set?

Using Personality Types in Goal-Setting

Besides factoring in the potential of each of your employees when helping them set and manage goals, you should also consider their personality type. All people have a different mix of abilities and talents, which influences what they want and how they go after it. This mix determines what motivates people, the risks they're willing to take, and the way they handle roadblocks and snafus. Personal development coach Rodger Constandse has identified four basic goal-setting personality types—or archetypes—that represent natural human tendencies and traits: the Warrior, the Explorer, the Diplomat, and the Scholar.

Though many people demonstrate characteristics of all four archetypes, most people tend to have a dominant style. Understanding your team members' personality types, Constandse says, will help you figure out the best way to work in your department to build on individual strengths and minimize their weaknesses as you set meaningful goals and strive to achieve them.

The Warrior. Focused and goal-oriented, warriors like challenges and risk but can be impatient with details and poor at planning, and therefore susceptible to "unexpected" problems. Their goal focus can make them forget their mission and overlook opportunities. Encourage them to write down goals, to plan and focus on the big picture, and to look for opportunities. Remind them about their dreams.

The Explorer. Good with people and moved by curiosity rather than by goals, explorers have broad horizons and big dreams—dreams so big that they seem impossible. Your job is to help them figure out what they want and how to get there. Write down the goals, plan, review them often, and help them prioritize and focus.

> "Only those who will risk going too far can possibly find out how far one can go."
>
> —T. S. Eliot,
> British poet
> (1888–1965)

The Diplomat. Skilled at building relationships, responsive, fulfilled by friendship and community, these strong team members are all about the people and the group. Your job is to help them focus on what their own needs and goals are. Encourage them to figure out what they want without allowing your expectations to influence their decisions.

The Scholar. The pursuit of expertise motivates scholars. Ability with details may mean they miss the larger picture, while their passion for being knowledgeable restricts their operations to their comfort zone. They may spend too much time planning and not enough doing. They need your help to develop long-term goals and plans for achieving them, and then to follow through. Urge them to take risks; show that failure won't bring disgrace. Praise their work ethic and high standards.

ORGANIZATIONAL AND INDIVIDUAL GOALS

The goals of each employee in an organization should converge so you're all moving in the same direction, instead of pulling against each other. The goals translate the corporate vision and strategy into individual objectives that are distinct, yet parallel.

The traditional model of a salesperson on commission illustrates how company goals can be relevant to individual employees. An experienced salesperson knows that trust is difficult to establish, so veteran sales staffers don't push unwanted products or services on a customer. They know that they will earn more from a loyal, repeat customer. In contrast, a new sales rep isn't going to care about long-term sales. This rep needs money and sales points now and is going to push the sale, even if it puts off a particular customer or customers permanently. The result is that this salesperson is always making a first sale—the hardest sale—and always struggling.

These two salespeople have the same goal and commission system, but there's a relevance gap. For the experienced salesperson, satisfying the customer is most important, because she knows long-term success will follow as a result. For the new sales rep, all that's relevant is getting his numbers up by closing sales, which drives completely different behavior and produces completely different results.

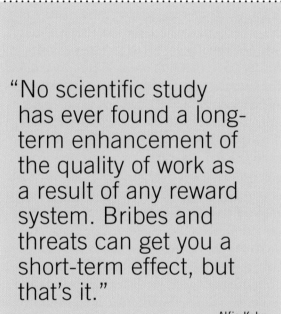

"No scientific study has ever found a long-term enhancement of the quality of work as a result of any reward system. Bribes and threats can get you a short-term effect, but that's it."

—Alfie Kohn,
author of *Punished by Rewards*

Just like the novice salesperson, many managers are driven by short-term results. Held accountable for the budget or sales performance for each quarter, there's no room for lower-than-expected results. All resources have to be pointed at pushing performance. But then the company goes into a crisis mode, stress levels rise, and, ultimately, the company's long-term progress suffers. A manager may understand the importance of the company's long-term goals and desperately want to pursue them, but the urgency of the need for short-term results mandates a different priority. A downward spiral ensues and it becomes progressively more difficult for the company to pull out of it. Manager stress increases, and their ability to do their jobs suffers.

Responsibility and accountability must go hand in hand. Too often, employees are given one without the other, which increases their feelings of helplessness and stress. Individuals often are held accountable for delivering results they can't control—outcomes that they don't have the authority or the responsibility to produce. For example, fast-food workers may be told their promotions depend on their ability to go three months without any customer complaints, yet they aren't empowered to make in-the-moment decisions that would calm an irate customer before a dispute escalated.

On the other hand, a worker might have responsibility for a function or logistical area, but is not be held accountable for bringing about the desired results. The fast-food worker might be assigned to resolve customer issues case by case, but have absolutely no reward or consequence for doing so. Initiatives may be launched

• POWER POINTS •

BEST PRACTICES BENCHMARKING

Benchmarking measures your company's methods, products, and services against those of the leaders in your field to identify "best practices." Benchmarking is a straightforward, chronological process:

- Decide what to benchmark.

- Determine whom to benchmark.

- Collect data.

- Analyze data.

- Draft "best practices" for your organization.

and responsibilities allocated, but many times the individuals responsible for making the changes aren't held accountable for meeting the objectives. Other changes occur, or more immediate requirements intervene, and the project slips on the agenda and then disappears. There's no reward for making the initiative happen, and no penalty for not making it happen.

Giving all employees the power and resources to make the successful outcome of a project one of their goals, and having them commit to a deadline, helps synchronize individual goals with those of the company. Holding employees accountable for achieving their part of the over-all company goal makes it relevant to them.

BEST PRACTICES: ACHIEVING GOALS

Within your organization, the discipline of benchmarking—measuring your products, ser-vices, and practices against the high standards set by competitors or leaders in the field—can help you identify best practices. The "best practice" idea is that one particular method or process is the most effective way to accomplish something and the best way to achieve results. By identify-ing the most efficient procedures and applying them to current goals and objectives, individuals and teams can quickly show improvement.

To integrate this method of benchmarking into the goal-setting and performance man-agement process, however, you need reliable, documented information about the whole range of your company's internal practices.

First you need to evaluate specific aspects of your organization's procedures in comparison to best practices outside your company. Second, you need to identify where your organization's procedures fall short and decide how you can improve them.

Organizational benchmarking is a powerful management tool that overcomes the insidious "the way we do it is the best way, because that's the way we've always done it" mindset. Bench-marking can inspire new methods, innovative ideas, and the creative use of existing tools. It can puncture resistance to change by showing the power of the alternatives used elsewhere. Sometimes such outside inspiration is needed to show how you can work smarter to achieve your goals.

MANAGING
GOALS

> "People with clear, written goals accomplish far more in a shorter period of time than people without them could ever imagine."
>
> —Brian Tracy,
> business consultant

Once you master the art of setting goals for yourself and your employees, it's critical that you learn how to manage those goals and create an environment in which you and your employees get results. Communication is essential to managing goals.

At every step in the process—setting goals, monitoring and encouraging progress toward meeting them, and finally measuring and rewarding success—you need to talk with and listen to your employees.

CREATING ACTION PLANS

Building and writing SMART goals are essential first steps, but execution—actually achieving

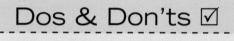

Dos & Don'ts ☑

GIVE THEM ALL THE HELP YOU CAN

Setting goals is only the first step. Once your employees have developed an action plan to achieve those goals, they need your encouragement and day-to-day support as they pursue it.

- ☐ Don't allow individuals to set vague goals that are too unstructured to achieve.

- ☐ Do encourage employees to drop activities that conflict with their goals.

- ☐ Do remind employees to work on achieving their goals every day.

- ☐ Don't let employees slack off; keep them focused.

- ☐ Do help employees get the resources they need to meet their goals.

those goals—is what is most critical. To help your individual staff members pursue their goals, you need to help them develop a vision of where they want to go—not only in the coming year but also in the long term. Then help them create an action plan to get there.

"Success seems to be connected with action. Successful people keep moving. They make mistakes, but they don't quit."

—Conrad Hilton,
founder of the Hilton Hotel chain
(1887–1979)

To create action plans, first meet with your staff and ask all employees to write down all the steps they must take to reach each goal by its deadline. Break down that list of steps into actions to be taken today, this week, this month, and in the coming months. This kind of incremental plan makes goals feel more immediate, more realistic, and more achievable.

Self-Assessment Quiz

THE GOAL-SETTING CYCLE

Read each of the following statements and indicate whether you agree or disagree. Then check your score at the end.

1. Competencies and performance goals are two different things.
   ○ Agree   ○ Disagree

2. I need to get my people to stop depending on my instructions.
   ○ Agree   ○ Disagree

3. Part of my mission as a manager is to train and develop people to replace me.
   ○ Agree   ○ Disagree

4. Empathy, self-awareness, supportiveness, self-control, and independence are good traits in my staff, and I should help develop them.
   ○ Agree   ○ Disagree

5. Managing goals and communication go hand in hand.
   ○ Agree   ○ Disagree

6. My reluctance to write things down is probably a drawback when it comes to goal-setting.
   ○ Agree   ○ Disagree

7. Personal development goals aren't usually a factor in performance evaluations

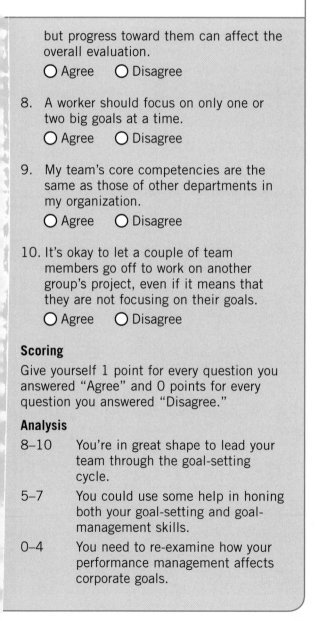

but progress toward them can affect the overall evaluation.

○ Agree ○ Disagree

8. A worker should focus on only one or two big goals at a time.

○ Agree ○ Disagree

9. My team's core competencies are the same as those of other departments in my organization.

○ Agree ○ Disagree

10. It's okay to let a couple of team members go off to work on another group's project, even if it means that they are not focusing on their goals.

○ Agree ○ Disagree

Scoring

Give yourself 1 point for every question you answered "Agree" and 0 points for every question you answered "Disagree."

Analysis

8–10	You're in great shape to lead your team through the goal-setting cycle.
5–7	You could use some help in honing both your goal-setting and goal-management skills.
0–4	You need to re-examine how your performance management affects corporate goals.

Help employees identify possible obstacles to accomplishing their goals and then develop action steps to avoid them. Always encourage your staff to face their fears. If your employees lack the skills to reach certain goals, build

• POWER POINTS •

TIME TO ADJUST YOUR GOALS

Change happens—and when it does, you need to modify your and your employees' goals accordingly. Some situations that might require you to revise goals and their corresponding action plans include:

- Changes in your company's industry or in the overall economy.

- Changes to your organization's business strategy and goals.

- Changes to your team's role or resources.

- Reorganizations in your business unit or department.

- An employee's acquisition of a new skill, immediately useful to the team.

- The early completion of a goal.

training into their action plan. Schedule some confidence-boosting, skill-building training courses and workshops, or arrange to have employees talk to experts or mentor with more knowledgeable colleagues.

> "You have to decide what your highest priorities are and have the courage— pleasantly, smilingly, nonapologetically—to say 'no' to other things. And the way to do that is by having a bigger 'yes' burning inside."
>
> —Stephen Covey,
> author of *The 7 Habits of Highly Effective People*

Make sure they take stock of the resources needed to reach their goals and the organizational procedures they'll need to follow to accomplish those goals successfully. Your own action plan should include becoming familiar with your company's resources and staff. Do you know how to procure additional supplies or acquire outsourced services? Your employees may need these resources and it is your responsibility to direct them to the right place.

Once an action plan is complete, employees should note the steps on their calendars or agendas so that the tasks become part of their daily focus. Remind them to allow time for unforeseen problems, delays, and revisions. Also make it clear that you expect them to shelve or reassign any activities that conflict with their goals or that don't contribute to the result they're trying to achieve.

Don't let employees get into the habit of saying they'll begin a project next week or next month. Urge each member to take some positive action toward a goal today and encourage them to check items off their to-do lists as soon as they complete them. This will not only record their progress, it will also give them a sense of accomplishment. Keep them focused on the benefits they'll receive—enhanced skills, job satisfaction, a sense of ownership—when they reach their goals.

Changing circumstances, such as a shift in job responsibilities or a new corporate mandate, might require you and your staff to modify the action plans you've drafted—or even the goal itself. Make any modifications using the same process you followed when you set the original goals and created their corresponding action plans.

MOTIVATING EMPLOYEES TO ACHIEVE

It takes vision, skill, and dedication to create a workplace where employees feel important and supported, and where they're committed to their work and to each other's growth and development. A team that's productive, innovative, and goal-oriented must be energized and fully engaged. If you don't intervene when your

NOT AN EMPLOYERS' MARKET FOREVER

In 2004, executive recruiting firm ExecuNet reported that 68 percent of the 278 employed executives they surveyed were unhappy with their jobs. Clearly, companies need to do better at keeping employees motivated and satisfied with their jobs. One way to accomplish this is by putting in place an effective performance management program that rewards employees for achieving goals. This is a significant workplace improvement that can be established without major expense or effort—and that can save you money on recruiting and hiring.

SOURCE: "Employees Don't Respond to Most Performance Plans" by Scott Cohen, *Wall Street Journal* (October 11, 2004).

THE BOTTOM LINE

talented employees' jobs have become routine, you run the risk of losing them, either physically or psychologically. You must stay on the lookout for opportunities to challenge each one of your employees.

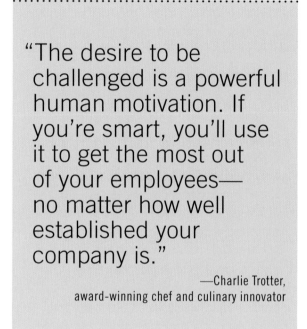

"The desire to be challenged is a powerful human motivation. If you're smart, you'll use it to get the most out of your employees— no matter how well established your company is."

—Charlie Trotter,
award-winning chef and culinary innovator

Workplace boredom is a major cause of employee turnover, which is expensive on several levels—it affects productivity, revenues, stock value, morale, public perception, and vulnerability to takeover. Unfortunately, it's often the smart and creative workers, the most valued employees, who become bored or restless the soonest. Because they are highly self-motivated, they tend to suffer in a company where innovation and action are discouraged. High achievers—and possibly perfectionists—in most aspects of their lives, they need stimulating goals, new challenges, opportunities for growth, and a stake in the organizational strategy. If good workers think their jobs don't provide these any longer, they may decide they've outgrown the company and start looking elsewhere.

On the flip side are those employees who are discontent because of a lack of job direction. Despite their potential, they do not stand out in the company. While they stay with the organization because it's convenient, they find ways to disengage. Rather than fully participating, they display counterproductive behaviors such as producing mediocre work, missing work routinely, and spreading a negative attitude around the office.

Your position as manager gives you the opportunity to energize both groups using goals. Let them set fresh goals and responsibilities or tackle them in ways that promote independence and innovation. Encourage them to handle new personal and group performance goals, and to rethink their contributions as part of the big picture. If they can challenge themselves to increase their knowledge and capabilities, they can envision a future at the company beyond today or this month.

Begin your energizing campaign by holding meetings with your team—first as a group to build team spirit and momentum, and then

individually to brainstorm the answers to these
questions:

- How do your goals contribute to the
  company's objectives?
- Which of your skills and abilities do you
  use at work?
- Which of your talents are untapped when
  working toward your goals?
- What aspects of your goals are challenging
  and rewarding?
- In what areas would you like more
  responsibility?
- If you could revise your goals or job
  responsibilities, what would you change?

Help your discontented employees renew
their energy and commitment to their jobs.
Several strategies are effective:

Expand teamwork. Form self-directed,
cross-department project teams. Give them the
freedom to set their goals, make decisions, and
allocate work as they see fit. Let everyone follow
through on projects from start to finish.

Switch tasks. Giving bored workers some
fresh goals can give them a lift and enrich their
skills—a benefit to your whole team.

Keep communicating. Make talking and
listening to your employees an everyday
occurrence, not just part of an annual ritual.
Employees want frequent input on how they're
doing, good or bad.

Broaden staff roles. Employees feel empowered when they can make decisions that affect
their work day—decisions about finances,
scheduling, or ways to juggle the whole group's

• POWER POINTS •

MOTIVATION

Motivation is key in setting and achieving goals. If you want your employees to perform, they must be dedicated and motivated.

- Hold regular meetings to set goals and encourage team spirit.

- Keep communication lines open at all times and listen to the comments and concerns that are raised.

- Engage employees in tasks that broaden their individual roles.

- Let your employees do the job they were hired to do by demonstrating confidence in their ability to perform well.

- To counter boredom, give creative employees stimulating goals and innovative challenges.

- Create projects that involve teamwork. Give teams the freedom to make decisions and set goals.

- Be supportive of their creative endeavors and bright ideas.

- Be a strong, supportive leader and you will have productive employees who will strive to meet goals.

work load. Another benefit of this level of involvement is that it highlights the big picture: employees learn that even the smaller decisions they make can support company goals.

Make creativity a buzzword. If you don't give employees the chance to think for themselves, they may lose their urge to be creative. Without it, they will quickly stagnate. Support creativity and reward bright ideas. Challenge your people with new goals, and give them the freedom and resources they need to achieve them. Support every idea. Many ideas that initially seem mediocre simply need modification to shine.

Another significant thing you can do as a manager to keep your employees energized and focused on meeting their objectives is to let them perform the jobs they were hired to do. Presumably you hired them for their skills and abilities, so allow them every chance to demonstrate—to you and to the organization—what they're capable of. Make it clear you'll supply any help they need. Listen to their comments as they go about tackling their goals: the more you listen, the better the job they'll do. Exhibit confidence in them and their ability to deliver. With a strong manager supporting them, employees will feel less pressure and are more likely to go above and beyond.

STAYING ON TRACK

Most goal-setting and performance management programs include procedures for written or verbal employee evaluation, or "formal feedback," at least once a year. However, monitoring your employees' progress toward their objectives and providing day-to-day feedback is just as important in helping them stay motivated and on track.

Monitoring Your Staff's Progress

One approach to remaining in touch with your employees and ensuring they are on track to accomplish their goals is "management by walking around." MBWA, as it is also known, was popularized by Tom Peters and Robert

Plan B

WALKING AROUND AFTER HOURS

One manager in an advertising firm had a smart riff on MBWA: "Walk the halls at 7:00 PM. It'll take you to the problem every time." His theory was that the people who were still at work at that hour were either committed employees working late to finish up a project or to clean up a colleague's problem, overwhelmed employees trying to sort out their own mess, or people avoiding a sorry home life. All of this can be very important for a manager to know.

SOURCE: *The Little Blue Book of Advertising* by Steve Lance and Jeff Woll (Penguin, 2006).

H. Waterman, Jr., in their best-selling book, *In Search of Excellence: Lessons from America's Best-Run Companies,* and is an easy practice to

Behind the Numbers

ROOM FOR IMPROVEMENT

Only 3 in 10 employees believed their companies' performance review system actually improved performance, according to a 2006 study by human resources consulting firm Watson Wyatt. Most said that what is measured has little to do with their actual jobs, that positive feedback is rare, and that even a stellar evaluation didn't result in a raise or bonus. In another Watson Wyatt study, nearly half of the employers surveyed said their managers were only minimally effective at boosting performance.

For their part, many employees resent the time they have to spend writing about and discussing potentially negative, touchy subjects. And because some companies use ambiguous evaluation and rating standards, employees often get little information on how to improve.

SOURCE: "Performance Reviews: Many Need Improvement" by Kelley Holland, *New York Times* (September 10, 2006).

put in effect as part of your daily management tasks. Rather than remaining barricaded in your office and observing or interacting with your staff only occasionally from across your desk, circulate among your staff's offices and cubes. Check in with them, ask questions, and respond to what you see. You will quickly learn who is busily ticking actions off a to-do list and who is staring into space daydreaming.

If it's true that the best work is created in a supportive environment, then your presence on the floor is a visible reminder of your support. Part social call, part fact-finding mission, MBWA allows you to mingle with your staff informally while checking on the progress of work.

Drop in when you know a staff member is available to talk, say, after the end of a phone conversation. After chatting about the local baseball team or last night's episode of a popular reality show, find out what your staffer really thought about the budget meeting earlier in the day. Then ask how the survey of the latest computer graphics applications is coming along, and recommend a Web site with pertinent product information.

In just one encounter, you've established rapport, gotten honest feedback on a meeting, determined the progress of a project, and offered a timesaving tip. After a few casual visits, your team will get to know you better and feel even more comfortable with you.

Does managing by walking around literally mean strolling the aisles? Not necessarily.

It could mean having a series of breakfasts, lunches or even fast-food runs with your employees, either individually or as a group. However you choose to reach out to your employees, it is critical to have daily contact with them—by phone calls, e-mailing, and staff meetings, as well as dropping by their offices for a few minutes. Don't interact with the same employees every time; vary your visits and the time you stop by. The point is to get to know your employees as people.

Make sure you listen to what your staff thinks about other key players in your organization—and they will likely have plenty to say. You will also hear what your team thinks about clients and other contacts outside the company, as well as what these clients say about your team. This is essential for managers who don't directly interact with these clients.

You can also pass on to your team, both formally and informally, what you're hearing on the managerial grapevine that might affect them. You can confirm good news, as well as squelch rumors before they escalate.

MBWA also gives you the chance to talk up your company's direction and goals—making them more integral to day-to-day operations—and to point out their relevance to your team's own goals. Encourage your staff to discuss new initiatives and policies that help them accomplish their goals.

So give yourself a break from meetings and e-mails and walk the halls a couple of times a week, not just when things are going well.

Providing Casual Feedback

By interacting with your employees daily, you keep information steadily flowing between

Dos & Don'ts ☑

GIVING EFFECTIVE FEEDBACK

Always give feedback as you monitor your employees' progress toward their goals.

☐ Do show your honest concern and appreciation.

☐ Do be timely about delivering praise, so that your employees see the direct connection between their actions and your response.

☐ Do praise in public, reprimand in private.

☐ Do give details about how things should change or why they need to continue as they are.

☐ Don't be judgmental; keep your comments objective.

☐ Do focus on specific behaviors.

☐ Do make time for discussion.

☐ Do keep a written record of what you agree on together.

yourself and your staff. Constant spontaneous feedback can reinforce productive behavior, energize unproductive employees, and improve negative attitudes. Providing frequent, casual feedback, in fact, is key to increasing your staff's ability to reach their goals.

"Ask, don't tell," is a smart approach to giving feedback casually. Simply asking an employee about a project or about a potential problem is often enough to open communication and invite the employee to seek your help if they need it. In response to your employees' answers, offer constructive feedback, without any implied threat.

Many supervisors believe they'll appear weak if they do too much asking; they assume that leaders should have all the answers. Yet you can enhance your own professional achievement and growth by asking your employees questions. You will not only understand their perspective and needs better, but you will also deepen your knowledge of their areas of expertise. In addition, asking questions goes a long way toward building trust. By showing an interest, you're also showing employees that they matter, something all workers desire.

Of course, there's a risk of being too casual. If you are overly offhand and friendly, some may misconstrue your intentions or, thinking you're a pushover, try to take advantage of you. Either situation undermines your authority and effectiveness. Be aware of the fine line between giving casual, honest, open feedback and being too friendly.

Casual feedback and monitoring not only strengthens your relationship with your staff and helps keep them focused on achieving their goals, it also paves the way for successful formal evaluations.

Evaluating Goal Achievement

"One way to keep momentum going is to have constantly greater goals."

—Michael Korda,
author of *Another Life*

In many companies today, honest, formal feedback and true goal-setting are all too rare. It's not surprising, then, that skeptics—from the rank and file to organizational behavior experts—question the value of performance reviews and call for their reform or elimination.

Still, many human resources executives and consultants believe that well-designed goals, continuing communication, and regular formal evaluations are essential for maximum employee performance and growth.

Unfortunately, many employees and their managers believe structured annual performance reviews are a nuisance at best, if not a complete waste of time. Many managers tend to dislike the annual review process: they believe it takes too long and that the paperwork is complicated, tedious, and redundant. In the end, they feel, nothing concrete comes of it. Often, individual raises are not linked to evaluation results or to company performance. All employees could be rated outstanding in their reviews, yet a company might be 15 percent below its revenue targets.

New managers, in particular, think of the performance reviews as a formidable task. They struggle to balance positive feedback—which helps employees improve their performance and enhance team output—with criticism—which might result in a decrease in morale, energy, and enthusiasm. Moreover, in some companies, performance evaluations are mostly about delivering bad news: about the department or the organization, about raises or the lack thereof, or about an employee's poor performance. "Get this thing over with," seems to be the overwhelming mantra on both sides of the desk.

Yet with the right approach, both you and your staff can look forward to the formal review process as an opportunity to advance goals and sharpen performance, recognize accomplishments, take stock, and make a fresh start.

Performance Evaluation Systems

A well-organized performance evaluation process can benefit everyone, from the employee to the manager, and even the customers and shareholders. In general, most companies evaluate all their employees at the same time at least once a year, although some organizations conduct performance reviews on the anniversary of an employee's hiring date. Twice-yearly or quarterly evaluations are becoming more popular

• POWER POINTS •

KEY PERFORMANCE RATINGS

Typically, the results of an evaluation are recorded on a standardized form. Many companies use the following simple three-point scale to rate an employee's competency and performance:

- **Excelled** – Goals and expectations were exceeded.

- **Fulfilled expectations** – Goals and expectations were met.

- **Needs improvement** – Goals and expectations were not achieved.

and are especially convenient and effective in fast-paced enterprises, where a more frequent, formal review of objectives is possible—and necessary.

Most companies evaluate their employees using a performance rating system. In this system, the employee is rated on specific and

EVALUATIONS CAN BE INDIVIDUAL OR COMPARATIVE

The two main performance evaluation methods rate employees either by a set of standards or by comparison with others. Several options further define each approach:

Individual evaluation methods – These performance evaluations require managers to rate individuals against defined standards, without comparison to other employees. Choice evaluation allows managers to use a set of descriptive statements about an employee. The critical incident method requires managers to keep a log of incidents of effective or ineffective performance for each person on their staff. In essay evaluations, managers write their own assessments of a worker's strengths and weaknesses.

consistent criteria on a scale typically ranging from "excellent" to "poor." This evaluation system can be easily standardized across the company, but some argue that it does not offer a complete picture of the employee's performance. Thus, many companies institute a modified rating system, which combines a

If a company uses a graphic rating scale, the oldest approach to performance evaluations, a manager scores the employee on a specific list of traits, assigning numeric or alphabetic ratings to each one.

Comparative evaluations – In the comparative approach to rating, managers compare all their direct reports to a list of desirable characteristics. One technique uses weighted checklists of objectives or of descriptive statements. Managers check off the item if they think the worker has met an objective or displayed a trait on the list. Otherwise, managers leave it blank. The employee gets a rating ranging from "excellent" to "poor" depending on the number of checks.

THE BOTTOM LINE

The BIG Picture

FORCED DISTRIBUTION AND LEGAL PROBLEMS

Forced performance rankings, or forced distribution—a brainchild of Jack Welch, former CEO of General Electric—gained momentum as a performance evaluation tool in the late 1990s. Forced distribution requires managers to assign a fixed percentage of their employees into distinct categories, such as "excellent," "acceptable," and "needs improvement." Those in the top category received the highest compensation and promotions. Those in the bottom ranking were likely to be denied increased compensation or promotion and were first in line to be laid off.

During its heyday, one in five large companies adopted forced distribution.

rating scale with a narrative description of an employee's performance.

Still, even those who accept the need for performance evaluations are wary of subjectivity or unfairness. As a result, some companies have devised alternative systems, some based on ranking or comparison, and others on assessments of the employee from many sources.

Paired comparison ranking systems involve pairing each employee with every other person

Within this system, formerly valued employees who had never had a questionable performance review found themselves at the bottom of departmental rankings—or out the door. Many in that situation were older, experienced workers who had built solid reputations in progressively more responsible roles. As a result, several large corporations ended up settling class-action claims in which former workers charged that disproportionate numbers of employees of a particular gender, age group, or racial designation had been fired.

SOURCE: "Forced Ranking and Age-Related Employment Discrimination" by Tom Osborne and Laurie A. McCann, *Human Rights Magazine* (Spring 2004).

on the team and designating the better performer in each pairing. Forced distribution, also known as "the curve" or "rank and yank," rates employees on the same type of curve used in classroom-grading systems. Many companies who climbed enthusiastically onto the forced-distribution bandwagon have jumped off, most notably Microsoft, where managers now put fixed percentages of individuals into categories that rate their potential to advance.

In the Roundtable method, members of one department or division discuss the employees in the group and their performance for the past evaluation period. They apply a curve and distribute the salary, bonuses, and promotions on the basis of the discussion.

Far more revealing are 360-degree reviews, which require observations from everyone who

360 DEGREES

Many employees believe the "360-degree feedback" method of evaluation paints a more accurate picture of their performance than feedback from their manager alone. A well-planned, well-managed 360-degree feedback process can be effective, but be aware of the pros and cons:

Pros
- Information is supplied by multiple sources and perspectives rather than from a single individual.

- Personal and organizational performance are integrated.

- Risk of discrimination is reduced, since feedback comes from varied sources.

works with the individual, including supervisors, peers, direct reports, and even customers. This method helps the employees understand how others perceive their performance.

In short, while performance evaluation systems may vary from organization to organization, they should all aim to measure an employee's ability to reach their goals in a consistent and fair way.

Plan B

- Customer service improves when feedback is solicited from internal or external customers.

Cons
- Compensation, promotions, and job longevity may be based on amateurs' assessments.

- Many supervisors have unrealistic expectations of 360-degree feedback.

- Because 360-degree reviews are often anonymous, there is no way to follow up for more information.

- Reviewers are not always objective and may focus on negatives or boost ratings to make someone look good.

- Paperwork increases when the number of participants escalates.

Red Flags ⚒◆

WHY PERFORMANCE EVALUATIONS SKEW

Certain standard problems tend to occur in evaluating the performance of a department or group of individuals. Be wary of making these judgment errors:

Central tendency error – The tendency to find all employees average and to assign average ratings to all areas of the evaluation form.

Contrast effect – The tendency to give lower ratings to an average employee who is evaluated right after an outstanding employee is.

Evaluation Pitfalls

Clarity, simplicity, and objectivity in performance review systems are the ideal, but putting theory into practice can be a challenge. Be aware of potential obstacles to effective goal-setting and performance evaluation.

The inherent flaw in any evaluation system is that ratings are typically based on opinions, and opinions are subjective. Some managers are generous in interpreting evaluation criteria, while others may be rigid and even stingy. Specialized training in observation and reporting

Halo effect – An unconscious attempt to give an employee ratings that match an overall impression or preconception you have of that person.

Leniency or harshness error – The tendency to view everyone as either good or bad.

Personal bias error – The tendency to give higher ratings to employees you like, or to employees who are generally well liked by others.

Recency of events error – The tendency to focus on more recent behavior and overlook past situations, whether positive or negative.

methods can improve a manager's ability to rate employees objectively.

The design and procedures of a company's rating system affect its success. If evaluation criteria are difficult to apply, if the procedures are cumbersome, or if the system seems to be more form than substance, participants are likely to disregard the whole process.

Conducting a Formal Evaluation

A performance review is a formal conversation and is therefore different from a casual chat

CASE *FILE*

FROM 'RATINGS CREEP' TO CUSTOMIZED GOALS

Several years ago, managers at St. Jude Children's Research Hospital in Memphis realized their performance evaluation program was suffering from "ratings creep." Supervisors had stopped using all but the top two of the five rankings available and so most employees had come to view the "meets expectations" ranking as negative. Moreover, the system was hard to apply uniformly among the various hospital groups—secretaries, researchers, doctors, nurses, and administrators.

St. Jude completely overhauled its system, replacing it with one that was easy to use and that worked well for everyone, while painting a clearer picture of how employees are doing. Managers work with each staff member to plan goals, and employees who do more are in line for special rewards and plum projects.

SOURCE: "Employees Don't Respond to Most Performance Plans" by Scott Cohen, *Wall Street Journal* (October 11, 2004).

in the hallway. For many new managers, their first performance evaluation means treading unknown territory. Conducting an evaluation is not simply a matter of saying, "I assume you've met all your goals" or, "If you didn't meet your goals, we have a big problem." Your job as a manager is to analyze the underlying causes that have led to the employee's success or failure and then communicate that to the employee so he or she can continue to improve and reach his or her objectives.

One reason managers say they hate conducting formal reviews is that they often involve confrontation. Who wants to deliver bad news and criticism, hurt someone's feelings, or be the object of animosity? It's easier to wait for the problems and issues to go away. But they rarely do. Being honest with an employee is far more effective than avoiding a discussion about that employee's underperformance. It's never a good idea to wait for your employees to figure out for themselves that they are not reaching their goals or that their performance is unacceptable. You must develop enough confidence in your leadership skills to address poor performance directly without feeling that you're delivering a personal attack.

If you've routinely provided casual feedback to your employees—for instance, noticing that a worker is preparing a report incorrectly and then demonstrating the right way to do it—it's unlikely that there will be any surprises during the formal evaluation. Knowing there won't be any unexpected issues raised during the review will keep your employees from being apprehensive or overly defensive—and should avoid most confrontations.

Instead, you and your employee can think of the formal review simply as a more structured version—scheduled and documented—of the day-to-day interactions and communications you already engage in. In this sense, the formal review can be experienced as just another work session, in which the focus is not on daily performance, but on the big picture and on updating or setting new goals.

Steps in a Standard Performance Evaluation

A performance evaluation based on goals—goals achieved and goals to be established—is a straightforward process. Follow these eight steps to schedule, conduct, and complete an effective performance evaluation:

Announce the reviews. Send out a group e-mail or other announcement about the upcoming performance reviews. Briefly emphasize the value of the process to your company, team, and individual employees. Mention that you look forward to your formal discussions and attach or enclose any paperwork you expect employees to fill out.

Schedule the appointment. Make an appointment to meet with each person on your team. If other managers in your division or department will review members of your team as well, schedule that meeting too. Make sure you allow plenty of time for the review.

These meetings should be free of interruptions and long enough to give your conversation the importance it deserves.

Compile data. Begin gathering data on each person you will be reviewing, such as your own observations, analysis of the employee's records, and notes of any discussions you've had with the employee or of conversations the employee engaged in with colleagues and supervisors. If you plan on incorporating 360 degree feedback, seek confidential input from the employee's coworkers, peers, and even customers if appropriate. Make sure to gather the information you will need to respond specifically to the evaluation criteria mandated by your company.

If other managers or supervisors will also review your direct reports, you must fully brief the reviewer on the employees' goals and objectives for the assessment period, their job descriptions, professional and personal development, and their projects, tasks, and special assignments.

Request self-evaluation. At the same time you begin gathering data, ask employees to complete a self-evaluation, measuring their own performance and their achievements relative to their goals and objectives. Also ask your employees to assess their own strengths and weaknesses, which can open a window into their self-perception and their own personal goals. Some employees are suspicious of formal self-evaluations, believing they could end up rating themselves too generously or too harshly. Let them know beforehand that the review is a

Outside the Box

COACHED TO ACHIEVE

Occasionally, when corporate budgets are flush and management believes a particular employee warrants an investment of time and money, the company hires a business coach. The move might be prompted by a specific problem, such as an employee's failure to meet a critical goal after a stellar performance history, or by complaints about the person's soft skills, such as anger management. The coach is hired to work with the employee to achieve a specified outcome in a given period of time.

Many employees are apt to be less than enthusiastic about the prospect of being

two-way street: any gaps between their assessments and yours will be discussed as part of the evaluation process.

Hold the review. Begin by sharing your general appreciation of the employee's progress toward achieving their goals, as well as their professional and personal development. Then discuss the specifics of the individual's performance. Acknowledge the completion of action plans and important tasks and the achievement of goals. Also discuss areas in coached, since it is often seen as an eleventh-hour alternative to dismissal. But whether coaching is intended to reclaim a problematic worker or to enhance a good worker's skills, those who complete a coaching program usually appreciate the experience.

Some employees who are at a professional crossroads hire a career coach or a "life coach" on their own, to help them work through roadblocks. Others develop a buddy system, partnering with a colleague at work or elsewhere to listen to and support each other and brainstorm ways to solve problems as they work toward goals.

which the employee's performance fell short and address any behavioral issues that get in the way of achieving your mutual goals.

Be honest and straightforward with your staff members. Treat them with respect and show that you are genuinely invested in their success, not just how it reflects on your own performance. Temper criticism with concrete, positive examples of how the employee can improve their performance. You want to encourage optimism about future success, even if things haven't gone

WORK **FLOW** TOOLS

EIGHT STEPS TO ACHIEVING GOALS

ANNOUNCE PERFORMANCE REVIEW PERIOD

MAKE APPOINTMENTS

GATHER FACTS

REQUEST SELF-EVALUATIONS

HOLD EVALUATION MEETINGS

SET NEW GOALS

SCHEDULE FOLLOW-UP MEETINGS

DOCUMENT EVALUATION MEETINGS

exactly as planned during the previous performance period. Don't forget to give employees a chance to share their self-evaluations.

The performance review is also a chance to emphasize your organization's expectations and values. Discuss key business objectives and reinforce the individual's contribution to meeting the overall corporate goals. With candor and clarity, communicate what you—and the rest of the company—expect from the employee. In addition, if your organization will be reassigning teams or individuals, the review meeting is an opportunity to discuss how the employee's ambitions and capabilities might best be used in the reorganized team.

Address goals. At the end of the review, develop goals and objectives for the next evaluation period. Goal-setting at the start of a new evaluation period may be as simple as adjusting and expanding the most recent goals to boost performance in the new cycle. If an employee has accomplished everything on the list, it may be time to set new goals and create a supporting action plan.

Make sure new and revised goals align with the organization's current strategy and parallel the individual's career path. For example, if your employee wants to learn how to run meetings, set goals that will require the employee to use that skill frequently or set a specific competency goal designed to develop that skill through coaching or formal training.

All your employees should leave the review meeting with clear, attainable goals and a shared understanding of how those goals will be measured. They should also have an action plan for each goal to guide them throughout the next evaluation period.

Set follow-up discussion. After the initial meeting, participants should consider the evaluation and comments on their own. Have any further discussion or clarification within a few days, while the original conversation is still fresh.

Submit review. Documentation is an integral part of the evaluation and goal-setting process. You should always provide a written evaluation—even if it is not required by your company—for each of your employees. Not only do written evaluations help track performance over time, they also provide a record of the employees' achievements that may help to justify recognition, reward, or promotion. This documentation also creates a paper trail in case an employee makes a complaint against you or it's necessary to terminate the employee.

For your written evaluation, complete your company's standard evaluation form—if there is one—or create your own. Regardless of the form you use, make sure you record any agreements that you made with the employee, including the goals and objectives you've set together for the following evaluation period. Some companies require the employee to sign the review form. Typically, the evaluation is filed with the next-level manager and the human resources department.

Difficult Evaluations

For many employees, evaluations are upsetting. Some people become morose and passive, or they get nervous and fidgety in anticipation of the review or during the review meeting. Some lose control of their emotions and become loud and angry. Others refuse to take responsibility for their poor performance and try to blame their coworkers. Still others push aggressively for a promotion or a raise, even to the point of threatening to quit. Perhaps the most difficult to deal with are the employees who don't accept any of your comments and argue every point.

Work at making the situation more comfortable right from the start. If staff members seem nervous or withdrawn, talk about a few non-work topics to set them at ease. As you move into the review itself, don't speak in terms of the person, but rather talk about the work and the job. Keep the discussion focused on your agenda and away from personality issues. Negative feedback, or criticism, is best handled in the same way as positive feedback—honestly and directly. Show your employees the respect they deserve by remaining calm and businesslike when you deliver a negative evaluation. Encourage an open dialogue between you and the employee—but be prepared for surprises.

Some people—most likely your more accomplished workers—will accept your evaluation, will be pleased at the positive feedback they received, and will agree to make the necessary changes to improve their performance. They are receptive to suggestions for training courses,

Dos & Don'ts ☑

DIFFICULT EVALUATIONS

A performance evaluation meeting creates a forum in which employers and employees alike can raise issues that may need to be addressed. They are as important for employees' personal development as they are to the growth of the company. Sometimes, employees are intimidated or feel uncomfortable with the process. Here are some ways to handle the difficult aspects of evaluations:

☐ Do try and create a comfortable and nonthreatening atmosphere when evaluating. This will help to put nervous or difficult people at ease when they are being evaluated.

☐ Do reschedule if you feel that an employee is not in an agreeable mood to handle being evaluated and receiving constructive criticism.

☐ Don't return an employee's hostile attitude; suggest that the evaluation be rescheduled for another day.

- [ ] Do keep your temper and emotions in check during a difficult evaluation.

- [ ] Do take the time to find out what is bothering a dissatisfied employee.

- [ ] Don't give into a dissatisfied employee's demands for a promotion or a raise if you don't feel that their productivity deserves special recognition.

- [ ] Do emphasize how valuable an employee is to the company if you feel she is about to accept another job offer.

- [ ] Don't focus on personality in the evaluation, but rather on performance.

- [ ] Do approach the evaluation process as a constructive way to deal with problems of which your employee may be unaware.

- [ ] Do listen closely and politely, but unemotionally, if an employee feels unappreciated, resentful, or angry.

additional responsibility, and new goals. But not every performance review is that easy.

If you are greeted by hostility or an oppositional attitude toward the evaluation process, suggest meeting on another day. The employee

The BIG Picture

CONTROVERSY OVER MONETARY REWARDS

Linking compensation to performance is based on the idea that rewards and bonuses motivate employees to excel. However, the value of incentive programs is debated. Do rewards help support corporate goals and foster collaboration, or do they generate unhealthy competition and conflict among employees? Some experts believe the more people are rewarded for doing something, the more they lose interest in the job itself and focus on the reward instead.

Rather than carrot-and-stick incentive programs, compensation should be part of corporate and team goals and strategy. Ideally, the organization is a community where employees participate in development and decisions and are fairly compensated in the first place.

simply may not understand the benefits of goal-setting and evaluation, and you'll have to explain their merits before you can conduct a successful review. Eventually the goal-and-review process will become a departmental value that most of your staff will accept and appreciate.

If you disagree on facts or on your evaluation of their performance, don't argue; try to diffuse it by suggesting you discuss the matter in your next meeting. Then, plan to gather more data for the next meeting and be prepared to state your case and stand your ground—but stay open to your employee's arguments and perspective. Be ready and willing to change your evaluation, if appropriate.

If an employee feels slighted or misrepresented, reschedule the meeting. Listen politely and intently. Stay friendly and collegial, and make a point of staying in contact and listening over the next few days. If an employee is in denial about a performance issue, try to find out why the employee can't see the problem the same way you can.

Employees who demand more money may not feel properly recognized for their work and may threaten to quit. Find out why they're unhappy. If their complaints relate to a specific problem, tell them you're already working on it, or will look into it immediately. If they bring up another job offer, discuss the advantages and disadvantages of each position, emphasizing how much you want to keep them on your team.

Remember to keep your cool no matter how emotional an employee becomes.

"The founder of a business gets to a point where his or her personal growth is much more involved with allowing others in the company to grow, so that they can give meaning to their own lives."

—Paul Hawken,
CEO of Smith & Hawken
and author of *The Ecology of Commerce*

Success and Failure in Meeting Goals

Rarely do employees completely "fail" to achieve their goals. More commonly, they accomplish some of the objectives they set out to meet. A programmer, for example, may complete four of the five actions needed to reach the goal of developing and launching a corporate intranet.

Or a salesperson may increase monthly client calls and resulting sales by 17 percent and 6 percent, respectively, when the goal was 18 percent and 8 percent.

Did these employees fail? Not exactly. The point of goal-setting is to define a target and the path to it, to grow and improve on the way to reaching it, and, ultimately, to contribute to the organization's forward movement. If goal-setting is viewed as a continuous process, then these employees did not fail. Goals are a road map to an employee's success. If employees takes a "wrong" turn or check out side roads on their journey, it doesn't mean they will never reach their destination. In fact, it could indicate that they are open to fresh ideas and innovations. Who knows what solutions they'll encounter along the way?

That's not to suggest employees can take any detour they want on their way to accomplishing their goals. Nor does it mean that they have built-in excuses for coming up short during evaluation time. But the goal and review process should be flexible and accommodating, especially given the rapid rate of change now standard in the workplace. Be ready to help your employees handle shortcomings and disappointments, along with acknowledging their achievements and setting new goals.

REWARDING GOAL ACHIEVEMENT

When a review confirms that a team member has accomplished his or her goals, then congratulations are in order—for your employee

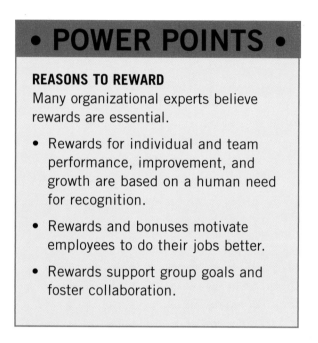

• POWER POINTS •

REASONS TO REWARD
Many organizational experts believe rewards are essential.

- Rewards for individual and team performance, improvement, and growth are based on a human need for recognition.

- Rewards and bonuses motivate employees to do their jobs better.

- Rewards support group goals and foster collaboration.

and for you. Goal-setting and performance management help you identify, develop, and keep these high performers.

The prevailing attitude among organizational behaviorists is that rewards should match performance. Most experts agree that a meaningful reward is an incentive to further achievement and improvement. Consequently, the top performers on your team should get more salary increases, bonuses, and other nonmonetary rewards. But even workers who have not been performing up to their potential, or who have fallen behind, need attention from management. For these employees, a system of rewards that recognizes "most improved" performance, for example, will sometimes increase their motivation and get them back on track.

One of the best ways to reward employees for achieving their goals is to give them special opportunities for training. Training helps motivate employees in general and specifically develops the technical and people skills that are essential for business. Core competency training, for example, enhances specific professional skills; service line training boosts functional skills. Training in a particular industry increases a worker's technical capabilities. Job-readiness training focuses knowledge and skill-building on specific projects; and internal forums, or "town halls," reinforce company values. High performers should be rewarded with additional training to add to their skills and knowledge and to prepare them for advancement.

MANAGING YOUR OWN GOALS

You've reviewed how to set goals with your staff, monitor their performance, spur productivity, evaluate their achievements, and reward effort. But what about your own goals?

While concentrating on your team's goal-setting and performance management, don't overlook your own goals and performance. Are your goals geared to supporting your people and improving their job performance? Do your goals support your supervisor's objectives and the mission of your company?

Managing and being managed simultaneously is a juggling act. You're accountable for your staff's performance as well as your own.

The more direct reports you have, the more precarious your position and the greater the likelihood you'll drop a ball—and you can bet someone will be watching when you do. Depending on the company, you may be judged on your abilities to:

- Motivate and engage your staff
- Collaborate with them, and provide assignments for their development
- Communicate and model the importance of goal-setting
- Set a positive direction and inspire your group
- Use resources efficiently
- Provide (and accept) feedback thoughtfully

Achieving Goals Can Get You and Your Company Where You Want to Be

Achieving goals is not about resting on one's laurels. The consumer wants a better mousetrap, a more efficient car, or a more nutritious cereal. To bring products to market, increase sales, or get the public's attention, innovations and improvements are an integral part of any cutting-edge company.

You want your company to succeed, but a company is only as good as its products and its employees. You want your employees to be productive, loyal, and happy. Statistics have found that replacing an employee costs well more than her salary; you must include lost productivity, hiring expenses, the training period for getting new personnel up to speed. Retaining top-notch employees, however, isn't just a matter of money.

Job satisfaction ranks high on the average person's list of employment benefits. Boosting your organization's ability to reach its goals is a winning way to maintain high morale and low employee turnover—and keep your company in business with a healthy bottom line.

Meeting goals is about your contented and high-functioning staff making your workplace attractive to clients and the general public, including prospective future employees. Having a productive work environment helps decrease employee turnover and increases efficiency, giving your company a much-needed advantage in this increasingly competitive global economy.

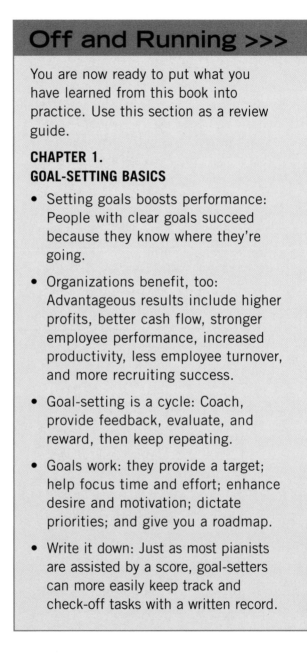

Off and Running >>>

You are now ready to put what you have learned from this book into practice. Use this section as a review guide.

CHAPTER 1.
GOAL-SETTING BASICS

- Setting goals boosts performance: People with clear goals succeed because they know where they're going.

- Organizations benefit, too: Advantageous results include higher profits, better cash flow, stronger employee performance, increased productivity, less employee turnover, and more recruiting success.

- Goal-setting is a cycle: Coach, provide feedback, evaluate, and reward, then keep repeating.

- Goals work: they provide a target; help focus time and effort; enhance desire and motivation; dictate priorities; and give you a roadmap.

- Write it down: Just as most pianists are assisted by a score, goal-setters can more easily keep track and check-off tasks with a written record.

- Don't be afraid: For goal-setting, the message is "nothing ventured, nothing gained"—not "nothing ventured, nothing lost."

- Be open and approachable: Instead of the command-and-control model, the modern manager should try to delegate and coach.

CHAPTER 2.
DEVELOPING GOALS THAT WORK

- Break it down: Dividing challenging goals into smaller ones can make even stretches attainable.

- Goals should be SMART: Specific, Measurable, Achievable, Realistic, and Time-bound.

- Make your goals effective: Target an objective; have a measurable outcome; include a specific finishing date and/or time; specify the outer limits of outlay in time, resources, and money.

- Be specific: Craft goals in clear, simple language. Effective goal statements inspire action.

Off and Running >>>

- Be realistic: A goal that is too far out of reach may discourage employees rather than motivate them.

- Set a deadline: Having a time frame for a goal gives impetus for advancing toward it sooner rather than later.

- Be flexible: Goals are not written in stone; if the overall business cycle or an individual's assignment changes, then performance goals must change, too.

- Set competency goals that allow people to develop "soft skills": Improved initiative and creativity, leadership and independence, people skills, productivity, quality, and responsibility make for a better overall employee.

- Reinforce your organization's culture and values: The goal-setting process allows for a discussion of the basic strategy of your company.

- Be ambitious: When setting long-term goals, try including one BHAG (big, hairy, audacious goal).

CHAPTER 3.
THE MANAGER'S ROLE IN SETTING GOALS

- Don't take a top-down approach: If employees at all levels of the organization help to create goals, then people will be more invested in setting and meeting them.

- Synchronize goals from one department or division to another: Working at cross-purposes won't help anybody.

- Goal-setting usually has three components: discussion; compromise or give-and-take; and agreement.

- Look at the big picture: Individual goals should make the greatest contribution to the overall plan.

- Individualize goals: Analyze the strengths and weaknesses of your employees, your organization, and yourself; find and focus on opportunities; and be aware of possible threats to your goal's success.

Off and Running >>>

- Accentuate the positive: Assigning team members tasks according to their strengths will achieve goals most quickly and efficiently.

- Consider personality type: Basic goal-setting personality types include the Warrior, the Explorer, the Diplomat, and the Scholar; work with them accordingly.

- Empower your employees: Give responsibility as well as accountability.

CHAPTER 4.
MANAGING GOALS

- Goals take work: After goals are set, create a list of steps to take to meet these goals, then create an action calendar or schedule to achieve your goals in a timely manner.

- Anticipate problems: Identify possible obstacles to accomplishing goals and then develop contingencies to combat them.

- Face fears: If employees lack skills, build training into their action plan.

- Achieving goals is personally rewarding: They produce enhanced skills, job satisfaction, and a sense of ownership.

- You can motivate your employees by expanding teamwork, switching tasks, keeping communication open, broadening staff roles, and making creativity a buzzword.

- Interact with employees daily: This allows the lines of communication to stay open between you and your staff, which yields better results.

- Ask, don't tell: Asking your employees questions shows that you're interested and that what they have to say matters.

CHAPTER 5.
EVALUATING GOAL ACHIEVEMENT

- Casual feedback and monitoring strengthens your staff: It helps them to focus on achieving goals and makes them more comfortable with evaluations.

Off and Running >>>

- Evaluations are not one-size-fits-all: The use of both individual evaluation and comparative evaluations can make for a clearer picture of an employee.

- Be fair: While performance evaluation can vary, it should always aim to measure an employee's ability to reach goals in a fair and consistent way.

- When doing performance evaluations, be aware of pitfalls: central tendency error, contrast effect, halo effect, leniency or harshness error, personal bias error, and recentness of events error.

- A formal review has a purpose: It can help a manager analyze underlying causes that have led to an employee's degree of success.

- A standard performance evaluation has the following steps: Announce the reviews; schedule the appointments; compile the data;

request self-evaluations; hold the reviews; address goals; set follow-up discussions; submit reviews.

- Not meeting goals is *not* "failing": If tasks have been completed to achieve an objective, then set a revised time frame or a more realistic benchmark for your goals and proceed; you're almost there!

- Don't forget your own goals: It's important to motivate and engage your staff, communicate effectively, use resources efficiently, and provide thoughtful—and constructive—feedback.

Recommended Reading

The Transparent Leader: How to Build a Great Company Through Straight Talk, Openness, and Accountability
Herb Baum with Tammy Kling
In the wake of numerous corporate scandals, Baum offers business leaders a compelling method to get maximum results by being open and honest in business practices.

Leaders: Strategies for Taking Charge, 2nd edition
Warren Bennis and Burt Nanus
Leadership guru Warren Bennis and his coauthor Burt Nanus reveal the four key principles every manager should know.

The Little Book of Coaching: Motivating People to Be Winners
Ken Blanchard and Don Shula
Renowned business consultant and best-selling author Ken Blanchard and legendary NFL coach Don Shula have motivated teams to peak performances. Here they share their secrets for inspiring others to greatness.

How to Win Friends and Influence People
Dale Carnegie
First published in 1937, this influential book offers time-honored advice on doing just what it says, proving that influencing other people in a positive manner can help you succeed in just about every endeavor.

Built to Last: Successful Habits of Visionary Companies
James C. Collins and Jerrold Mundis
Groundbreaking research provides new insights into the creation and maintenance of the most enduring and successful companies.

Flow: The Psychology of Optimal Experience
Dr. Mihaly Csikszentmihalyi
In this best-selling introduction to his landmark "flow" theory,
Dr. Csikszentmihalyi interviews almost 100 creative people
from a wide array of fields to explore the creative process and
shows the benefits of creative thinking on one's quality of life.

*The 7 Habits of Highly Effective People: Powerful Lessons in
Personal Change*
Stephen R. Covey
First published in 1990, this best seller shows you how to
change your mindset to adopt these important habits for success. Translated into thirty-two languages, this book has sold
more than 10 million copies.

*The Strategy Machine: Building Your Business One Idea at a
Time*
Larry Downes
The tools in this book will teach you how to innovate on a
daily basis and how to profit from the transformation going on
right now in your industry.

The Effective Executive
Peter F. Drucker
Drucker shows how to "get the right things done," demonstrating the distinctive skill of the executive and offering fresh
insights into old and seemingly obvious business situations.

Innovation and Entrepreneurship
Peter F. Drucker
This is the classic business tome for presenting innovation
and entrepreneurship as a purposeful and systematic discipline. This practical book explains what all businesses and
institutions have to know, learn, and do in today's market.

The Practice of Management
Peter F. Drucker
The first book to depict management as a distinct function
and to recognize managing as a separate responsibility, this
classic Drucker work is the fundamental and basic book for
understanding these ideas.

*The Daily Drucker: 366 Days of Insight and Motivation for
Getting the Right Things Done*
Peter F. Drucker with Joseph A. Maciariello
Drucker offers his penetrating and practical wisdom with his
trademark clarity, vision, and humanity.

*Five Frogs on a Log: A CEO's Field Guide to Accelerating
the Transition in Mergers, Acquisitions, and Gut Wrenching
Change*
Mark L. Feldman and Michael F. Spratt
Designed for corporate managers and CEOs caught up in the
whirlwind of change, every chapter provides accessible ideas
and wisdom for navigating the most demanding business tran-
sitions.

How to Sell Anything to Anybody
Joe Girard
"The world's greatest retail salesman" *(Guinness Book of
Records)* shares his secrets for finding customers, closing
deals, and making lifelong friends.

The Ecology of Commerce: A Declaration of Sustainability
Paul Hawken
The entrepreneur behind the Smith & Hawken gardening supply empire proposes an Earth- and people-friendly approach to
business.

"Yes" or "No": The Guide to Better Decisions
Spencer Johnson, M.D.
Best-selling author Spencer Johnson presents a practical system anyone can use to make better decisions in both one's
professional and personal life.

*Punished by Rewards: The Trouble with Gold Stars, Incentive
Plans, A's, Praise, and Other Bribes*
Alfie Kohn
Seeing rewards as bribery, the author argues that teamwork,
meaningfulness, and autonomy are incentive enough for both
students and workers.

Leading Change
John P. Kotter
Kotter shows how executives at all levels need to address and
lead the organization by improving the status quo.

Swim with the Sharks without Being Eaten Alive: Outsell, Outmanage, Outmotivate, and Outnegotiate Your Competition
Harvey B. Mackay
In this straight-from-the-hip handbook, with almost 2 million in print, best-selling author and self-made millionaire Mackay reviews the secrets of his success.

You Can't Win a Fight with Your Boss: & 55 Other Rules for Success
Tom Markert
This guide to surviving the pitfalls of the modern corporate environment presents fifty-six practical rules that one can use to find corporate success.

The Corporate Coach: How to Build A Team of Loyal Customers and Happy Employees
James B. Miller with Paul B. Brown
Founder and CEO of Miller Business Systems, Jim Miller shows how giving customers legendary services and also motivating employees makes for a winning combination.

Launch It!: How to Turn Good Ideas into Great Products
Molly Miller-Davidson, JoAnne Stone-Geier, and Michael B. Levinson
Written by an expert team of trend and product consultants with over sixty years of collective experience advising thousands of entrepreneurs, designers, and companies, this book provides step-by-step nuts-and-bolts advice.

In Search of Excellence: Lessons from America's Best-Run Companies
Thomas J. Peters and Robert H. Waterman, Jr.
Based on a study of 43 of America's best-run companies, *In Search of Excellence* describes eight basic principles of management that made these organizations successful.

Emily Post's The Etiquette Advantage in Business, 2nd edition: Personal Skills for Professional Success
Peggy Post and Peter Post
Helpful guidance for appropriate behavior and communication for both everyday and unusual situations essential to professional and personal success.

Quiet Leadership: Six Steps to Transforming Performance at Work
David Rock
Rock demonstrates how to be a quiet leader, master at bringing out the best performance in others, by improving the way people process information.

Writing That Works, 3rd edition: How to Communicate Effectively in Business
Kenneth Roman and Joel Raphaelson
This completely revised and updated edition shows how to say what you have to say more succinctly and with less difficulty and more confidence.

Overcoming Underearning ™: Overcome Your Money Fears and Earn What You Deserve
Barbara Stanny
Filled with inspiring, real-life stories of underearners who turned their lives around, Stanny provides a message of empowerment and hope to those who chronically undervalue themselves.

Sun-Tzu: The New Translation
Sun-Tzu and J. H. Huang
Popularly known as *The Art of War, Sun-Tzu* is one of the leading books on strategic thinking ever written. Now in a ground-breaking translation based on newly discovered material.

Radical Collaboration: Five Essential Skills to Overcome Defensiveness and Build Successful Relationships
James W. Tamm and Ronald J. Luyet
To get what you need from the world around you, Tamm and Luyet teach you how to reach your goals by using the highly effective interest-based approach to problem solving.

You Will Be Satisfied
Bob Tasca with Peter Caldwell
The owner of a small Ford dealership with the world's greatest sales volume shows how anyone can drive customer loyalty to produce results.

The Cycle of Leadership: How Great Leaders Teach Their Companies to Win
Noel M. Tichy
Using examples from real companies, Tichy shows how man-

agers can begin to transform their own businesses into teaching organizations and better-performing companies.

The Leadership Engine: How Winning Companies Build Leaders at Every Level
Noel M. Tichy
A framework for developing leaders at all levels of an organization helps to create the next generation of leaders so that a company can grow from within, which is the key to excellence, stability, efficiency, and building team loyalty.

The Visionary's Handbook: Nine Paradoxes That Will Shape the Future of Your Business
Watts Wacker and Jim Taylor with Howard Means
This book presents a vision of the present and future to create a course for the future based upon the authors' understanding of nine paradoxes that define the business and social climates of the world.

Winning
Jack Welch with Suzy Welch
The core of *Winning* is devoted to the real "stuff" of work. Packed with personal anecdotes, this book offers deep insights, original thinking, and solutions to nuts-and-bolts problems.

Index

Make sure you have all the Best Practices!

COLLINS BEST PRACTICES

Achieving
GOALS

Define and Surpass Your
High Performance Goals

KATHLEEN SCHIENLE

Best Practices: Achieving Goals
ISBN: 978-0-06-114574-2

COLLINS BEST PRACTICES

Communicating
EFFECTIVELY

Write, Speak, and Present
with Authority

GARRY KRANZ

Best Practices: Communicating Effectively
ISBN: 978-0-06-114568-1

COLLINS BEST PRACTICES

Difficult
PEOPLE

Working Effectively with
Prickly Bosses, Co-Workers,
and Clients

JOHN HOOVER

Best Practices: Difficult People
ISBN: 978-0-06-114559-9

COLLINS BEST PRACTICES

Evaluating
PERFORMANCE

How to Appraise,
Promote, and Fire

BARRY SILVERSTEIN

Best Practices: Evaluating Performance
ISBN: 978-0-06-114560-5

Make sure you have all the Best Practices!

COLLINS BEST PRACTICES

Managing
PEOPLE

Secrets to Leading for
New Managers

BARRY SILVERSTEIN

Best Practices: Managing People
ISBN: 978-0-06-114556-8

COLLINS BEST PRACTICES

Motivating
EMPLOYEES

Bring out the Best in
Your People

BARRY SILVERSTEIN

Best Practices: Motivating Employees
ISBN: 978-0-06-114561-2

COLLINS BEST PRACTICES

Time
MANAGEMENT

Set Priorities to Get the
Right Things Done

JOHN HOOVER

Best Practices: Time Management
ISBN: 978-0-06-114563-6

COLLINS BEST PRACTICES

Hiring
PEOPLE

Recruit and Keep
the Brightest Stars

KATHY SHWIFF

Best Practices: Hiring People
ISBN: 978-0-06-114557-5